HOW TO MAKE A LIVING.

How to Make a Living

SUGGESTIONS UPON THE ART OF MAKING SAVING, AND USING MONEY

BY

GEO. CARY EGGLESTON

Author of "How to Educate Yourself," etc., etc

NEW YORK
G. P. PUTNAM'S SONS
27 AND 29 WEST 23D STREET

PREFACE.

THIS little manual makes no literary pretensions whatever. In preparing it, I have been concerned only for its practical usefulness, and I send it to press asking for it no other consideration than that which its teachings may be found to deserve.

The need of such a volume of homely hints upon practical matters was first suggested by the numerous letters of inquiry which came to me from all parts of the country, during the period in which I conducted a household weekly paper, and there is hardly a paragraph in the following pages which is not in some sort a reply to more than one earnest question. If the answers given shall prove of advantage to the questioners, and to others in like circumstances, the little book will have done its whole duty.

CONTENTS.

HOW TO MAKE A LIVING.

CHAPTER I.

THE VALUE OF MONEY.

ITS RELATION TO OTHER THINGS.

EVERY bookkeeper knows that tyros in his business find nothing so difficult of comprehension as the nature of cash and its place in the economy of mercantile affairs. It is difficult to make the student of accounts understand that cash comes by purchase quite as truly as any other merchandise does, —that what money one gets one must pay for, and that there is an exact limit to the value of dollars and cents, which must be kept in mind in purchasing money with other things, just as the value of other things must be kept in mind when they are to be bought with money. With the young bookkeeper, however, the difficulty is a technical one principally, and is soon mastered; while the rest of us are apt to blunder on through life with a very faint conception, or no conception at all, of the real relation of money to other things. The trouble comes from the fact that we express values usually in terms of money, and so we come to regard dollars and cents as of fixed and certain value,—as constituting an invariable standard by which to measure everything else. A unit of measure gets to be, in some sort, an ultimate fact; and we take it as a starting-point. The pound, the foot, the gallon,—these we know are fixed measures, and, understanding them, we do not care, commonly, to go behind them with inquiries of any sort. And we are apt to place the dollar in precisely the same category of fixed things; assign to it a certain value; and, while we measure everything else by it, let it go without any measurement at all.

ITS VALUE NOT A FIXED ONE

In point of fact, however, money is not of fixed and certain worth at all. I speak, now, not of paper promises to pay, which are always reducible to their value in gold, but of gold itself. When the gold dollar will buy two bushels of wheat, and other things in proportion, it is really and truly worth just twice as much as it is when it will buy but one bushel. In other words, its purchasing capacity is the real measure of its value. Now, this purchasing capacity varies in different countries and at different times in the same country; wherefore, it is evident, the real value of money varies at different times, and in different places quite as truly as does the value of any other article of commerce. And it varies for precisely the same reason, too. If the cost of production,—*i. e.*, the amount of labor necessary to the production of a given quantity of gold,—be increased or diminished without a corresponding increase or diminution in the cost of producing other things, the purchasing power (which is the value) of gold undergoes a change at once. And if for any reason the cost of producing other articles of daily use be enhanced or diminished, without a corresponding change in the cost of gold production, there must be a proportionate change in the value, as there is in the purchasing power of gold. We cannot always trace these results to their ultimate causes, for the reason that there may be, and usually is, a complexity of cause which baffles us, but we know the fact nevertheless, that the value of money is measured by its purchasing power,—in other words, that money is worth just what it will buy—no more and no less.

All this seems simple enough, and yet it is a fact constantly overlooked, and forgetfulness of it is a fruitful source of error on the part of individuals as well as of communities, and it is necessary, for the purposes of this little book, that the reader shall impress upon his mind in the outset this truth, that *money is an article of varying value, worth what it will buy, and no more.*

THE COST OF MONEY.

It seems a sufficiently evident truth that we cannot afford to pay more for any article than it is worth, and in most of our dealings we bear this truth in mind,—but how many of us are there, who distinctly and constantly recognize the fact that we must pay for what money we get, and that we cannot afford to pay more than it is worth? We constantly forget that we get literally nothing in this life without paying for it in some way. If we read a book for the sake of the information, or the culture, or the amusement it is capable of giving us, we must pay for what we get, in a valuable commodity, *time*. If the time spent in reading be worth less to us than the culture, or the information, or the amusement which the reading brings, we do well to purchase at the price,—to give the thing of smaller for the thing of greater value. And this is true of everything else. We cannot have money, or friends, or culture, or ease, or comfort, or amusement, or pleasure, or any other desirable thing whatever, without paying, in one way or another, for what we get; and so it becomes our duty in every case to learn accurately the value of the coveted thing, and the price we must pay for its possession. If the price be too high, we should forego the desired good, as one which we cannot afford to buy. If, on the other hand, the thing wanted is to be had at a sufficiently small cost, we do well to buy it. It is not enough that the thing wished for shall be a good and desirable one. It must be better and more desirable than that which we must give in exchange for it, or we cannot afford to purchase it at all. Books are good things, doubtless, and so are pictures and statuary. Comfortable homes are of great worth. Travel is an excellent educator. All these and a hundred other things are desirable certainly, but they can only be had at a certain cost in time or money, or both, and the question whether or not we should have them, depends wholly upon that other question, whether or not they are worth to us more than their cost. There is no doubt of their desirability, but it is not every one who can afford them.

What is true of all these things is true also, and equally, of money. It is worth something, certainly. It is worth a good deal, too, but it is not worth everything. It is a good thing to have, but it is not the only good, or even the chief good, to be sought in life. Each of us needs it, and some of it we must have, but there is a limit to the amount of it which we can afford to buy, and beyond that limit we may not wisely go. The trouble is, commonly, that we think and talk about *making* money, when in point of fact we do nothing of the kind. Whatever money we get in the world we *buy* quite as truly and quite as directly as we buy the clothes upon our backs. Every man begins life with certain possessions. These are his muscles, his intellect, his skill at work of any kind, his education, his health, his energy, his character and whatever property he may happen to have inherited. With these he must buy whatever desirable things he gets in life,—books, houses, lands, money, and everything else. If he be a wise man he will take care not to pay more for any of these than he can afford; but few of us, unfortunately, are wise in this regard. Knowing very well that we may live and be comfortable with small possessions, in the way of money and property, we, nevertheless, overwork ourselves now and then,—paying in precious health a price we cannot afford to pay, for money that we really do not need; or we sacrifice something of character for the sake of increasing our purchases of things which are of infinitely smaller worth; or we starve our intellects that we may buy more wealth, becoming poor, that we may seem to be rich. There are a hundred ways in which we are constantly liable to make bad bargains in purchasing wealth, and the very first lesson in economy is this: *Be careful that you do not buy money, or its equivalent, at too high a price.*

There are very few people who do not feel the need of more money and property than they have, and feeling this daily and hourly, it is only natural that we should come to think of money, which is the representative of all property, as of greater worth than it is. We are in constant danger, therefore, of buying it at too high a price, and from first to last there is nothing more essential than that we shall avoid this error. To do this, each of us must determine, from time to time, how much money he can afford to make. Beyond the necessity of providing for his own and his family's absolute wants, the making of money becomes a mere question of one's ability to buy. "I have not time to make money," said Agassiz, and with all his ability to amass a fortune almost without effort, he died owning nothing except his library and a mortgaged homestead. The making of money would have been very easy to him. His vast store of knowledge might have been turned into popular books and lectures, almost without labor, and money would have flowed into his lap. He had need of money, too, and could have used it to better advantage than most men can. But he could not afford to buy it. The cost he must pay for it was time, and he felt that to be more precious than anything else. His hours were worth more than the money they would buy, and he, being a wise man, refused to purchase at a price which he thought too high.

Time is not so valuable to every man as it was to him, but time is not always the only thing one must pay, and there are but very few of us who do not, in one way or another, pay too high a price for the money we get in the world,—very few who do not buy more money than they can afford, and there is no worse extravagance possible than this.

Each of us has certain aspirations in life. There are certain things which each of us would like to accomplish, and for the accomplishment of which the possession of money is necessary. For the most part these aspirations are worthy ones, or at least not unworthy. But their accomplishment is not absolutely necessary—if we be rightly constituted people—even to our own happiness, and we must be careful not to let our zeal for these things mislead us as to their value and the value of the money necessary to their accomplishment. But above all we should never forget that while money is an excellent means, it never can be a worthy end. It is an excellent servant, but the worst of all possible masters. It strengthens our hands for all purposes, but has no value whatever except in its use.

Now we all know precisely what money will purchase, and so we have an exact measure of its worth constantly at hand. We know that a given amount of it will enable us to live in a certain way; to have certain comforts and luxuries; to indulge certain tastes; to relieve a certain amount of distress; to accomplish certain desired ends. Knowing this, and knowing precisely how desirable it is to live in this way, to have these comforts and luxuries, to indulge these tastes and to accomplish these ends, we have only to ascertain precisely how much of economy and of labor, how much of self-sacrifice, how much of the sacrifice of those dependent upon us, we must give,—in short, what price we must pay for these things, to know whether or not we can afford them. If we can accomplish the ends we have set before us at reasonable cost, we should do so by all means. If we cannot, then we have no right to accomplish them at all. We are, in that case, precisely in the predicament of a man who wishes to live in a costly, well-appointed house, but is without the money necessary to pay for the luxury.

TOO MUCH MONEY.

The truth is that most of us make more money than we can afford. We begin by spending too much, indulging extravagant tastes, and living in a style which requires not more money, perhaps, than we can make, but more than we can afford to make. In order that we may do this we overtax our strength in work; deny ourselves needed rest; pinch our souls in a hundred ways; impoverish our minds; deny ourselves the advantages of reading, leisure, study and travel; and sometimes cut short our lives. Can there be doubt that, in all such cases, we pay more for the thing we get than it is worth?

It should be our care, then, not to set before ourselves too great a task in life. We should begin with small ends in view, and allow our purposes to widen when the means for their accomplishment shall be ours. We should beware of creating an artificial necessity for money, lest that necessity leads us to buy the commodity at an extravagant price.

In this, as in everything else, it is of the utmost importance that we shall decide in advance what we intend doing in life. A vague purpose to make a good deal of money, and do a good many other things, is about the worst one with which it is possible to begin life. As a rule, he that does two things will do neither well, and it is important that every young man shall determine precisely to what end he will live. Without doubt,

Mrs. Barbauld spoke truth when she said, that "any man may become rich if he chooses to pay the price," but the price is usually a very high one. In this country, one can make money in considerable quantities, if he devote himself to the task to the exclusion of everything else, but it is by no means easy for one to become rich, while he is accomplishing anything else. If you would become learned, your time and your energies must be given to the task of acquiring knowledge. If you desire to make a name for yourself, you must add attention and industry to what talent or genius you may have, and pay the whole for the reputation you seek. If you would be rich, you must deny yourself all other good things,—you must give your days and nights, your thoughts, your energies, to the making of money; you must restrain your hand when you would be generous in almsgiving; you must deny yourself luxuries and comforts; you must forego most of the pleasures of life, and devote yourself wholly to the one task of getting and keeping money. This is the price which most of us must pay if we would be rich, and it is the price, too, which most men, who have become rich, have paid.

There are exceptional cases now and then, but they are too rare to be taken into the account in this place. *As a rule*, one must forego the thought of becoming rich, if he would accomplish anything else in the world, and the choice ought to be made at the start. The trouble is, that many of us are constantly trying to get wealth and hoping to get it, while we steadily refuse to pay the price. We even allow ourselves to grow unhappy, sometimes, over our failure to get that for which we deliberately refuse to pay. We live in a style which we can well enough afford, perhaps, but which precludes the possibility of amassing a fortune; we indulge tastes which are altogether commendable, but which cost us a good deal in time, money, attention or energy; we open our hands to the needy, as we ought, but as we cannot afford to do if we are to become rich; we pursue studies which enrich our minds, at cost of neglecting the getting of money; we entertain our friends, and keep our families in comfort, which is right and proper, but is not at all the way to make a great deal of money; and having thus used our means in buying innumerable other good things, we grumble at our inability to purchase that wealth for which, if we are to have it at all, we must forego all these things. Nothing is commoner than this, and nothing could be more unreasonable. We cannot eat our cake and have our cake, and it is the part of wisdom to decide whether we shall eat or keep it. If you set wealth before you as the object of life, the way is open and evident to the attainment of your end. You have only to surrender all other objects. Work without regard to anything else. Make all the money you can, and keep all you make. Stint your body and starve your mind and soul. The mere accumulation of money by these means is easy and certain, but the price you must pay is an outrageously high one. Yet it is the price which ninety-nine men in a hundred must pay if they would have wealth.

It is far better to abandon the idea of getting rich and to devote one's self to a higher purpose from the beginning. But some money we must have, and the question each should decide for himself in beginning life is, *How much money can I afford to make?* The answer will depend upon several other things.

In the first place, you must ascertain what your money-making capacity is,—not in a vague, uncertain way, but positively. Knowing this you must determine also how much money you will be required to spend, in living as you purpose living, and the difference will be the amount you can afford to save. An intelligent conception of one's purpose in life, kept steadily in view, will go a great way toward solving the problem of happiness or misery. It puts an end to vague longing and precludes discontent. It enables one to accomplish, at least approximately, the end he has set before him, and so makes of him a satisfied instead of a disappointed man. It puts fancy in harness and makes her help to draw the load.

CHAPTER II.

THE DUTY AND THE DANGER OF MAKING MONEY.

THE LIMIT OF ONE'S RIGHT TO MAKE MONEY.

HAVING determined how much money you are capable of making,—how much you wish to make, and how much you can afford to make, it remains to be decided how much you have a right to make, for in this every man is subject to a limitation which he may not transcend without wronging himself and defrauding the world of its just dues. There can be no more positive error than the common thought, that every man has a right to make all the money he can by honest methods. Life brings duties with it, as well as privileges, and every man owes the world a debt which he must pay if he would be truly and perfectly honest. To refuse payment in this case is as positively a failure in honesty as to neglect it in any other. Every man owes it to the world to do the very best work of which he is capable. We live in daily enjoyment of a civilization wrought out by those who have gone before us, and in enjoyment also of the results of the work done by our fellows still living. The world gives us all these things, and in return we cannot honestly refuse to render our own best service. Disguise the fact as we may, the family of mankind is a community, each individual sharing, in one way or another, in the work of all the rest.

No man has a right, therefore, to devote himself so exclusively to the task of making money, as to neglect the doing of his best work in the world, or to unfit himself for its doing. The force of this is felt most strongly when one comes to determine what his business shall be. Professor Agassiz was bred a physician, and might have made the practice of his profession much more lucrative than he could ever hope to make the work he chose to do in the world. But while he might have been a useful and prosperous man, writing prescriptions in some European city, he would, in that case, have defrauded the world not only of the scientific discoveries he made, but also of the museum at Harvard, one of the completest natural history collections in the world, which was built up almost exclusively by his skilled labor. We should have lost, too, the influence he has exerted upon the educational system of our country; the school at Penikese; the hunger and thirst for scientific information which are working a revolution, not in our schools only, but in our lives as well. The world would have lost all these merely that Louis Agassiz might accumulate a few thousands of dollars. And the rule we apply to his case is applicable to all. It is given to few men to accomplish the tenth part of that which he did, but every man may do far more if he choose his work wisely and conscientiously, than if he determine it merely by the test of its pecuniary productiveness.

Besides the general duty of every man to do the work for which nature has best fitted him, every man owes it to himself so to choose his business as to secure the largest intellectual and moral growth, and the greatest degree of happiness to himself and to those around him. All these things should have their weight not only in the choice of a business, but equally in its pursuit, and all these things limit the right of a man to make money.

THE GENERAL RULE.

The general principle involved may be stated in a few words, as follows: *It is the duty of every one to make money enough to supply the reasonable wants of himself and of those dependent upon him. It is his privilege to make as much more as he can without sacrificing worthier ends.* The application of this principle will be seen in subsequent chapters, and in its application to individual cases it leads to various results. It prompted Agassiz, as we have already seen, to forego the easy accumulation of money in order that he might do that work for which he was so eminently fitted, and which the world so greatly needed. On the other hand, such men as Stephen Girard and Peter Cooper have been impelled, by identically the same principle, to the laborious accumulation of enormous wealth, as the implement with which alone their equally excellent work might be done. Had Agassiz made money, his work must have been neglected. To Girard and Cooper the making of money was an essential part of the task set them.

SOURCES OF ERROR.

There are so many pleasant things connected with the possession of wealth, and man is so prone to think those things good which are agreeable, that every one of us is in danger of magnifying both the duty and the privilege of accumulation.

We are apt to think ourselves best fitted for those things at which we can most readily, and most surely, make money, and here is a danger to be avoided. Without doubt, our ability to make a calling profitable is, in some sense and to some extent, a measure of our fitness for it; but that it is not always a correct measure is evident. There is another danger, too, to be guarded against, namely, that as our accumulations increase, the desire to accumulate will grow with them, until it becomes a genuine passion, in which case it is sure to override every other consideration, and make of us mere machines for making money, than which no fate can well be worse. The birth and growth of this passion is almost always imperceptible, and hence the danger is one which can be guarded against only by the utmost watchfulness of an alert conscience. To avoid it with certainty, one must keep constantly in view the purposes for which he is making money, never allowing himself for a moment to regard the money itself as an end worth working for.

These general principles are not in any sense new. They have been stated so often that I should gladly omit them here but for the fact that they are constantly neglected in practice. Upon them rests the whole body of the ethics of money-making, which, in our country at least, involves almost all there is of ethics. Their statement here is necessary, too, as a foundation for what follows. It is necessary for the reader to understand, in the outset, the point of view from which we are to consider our subject, and to this end I recapitulate the principles upon which this little treatise rests, as follows:

1. It is both the right and the duty of every man to make

money enough to supply the reasonable wants of himself and his family.

2. It is the right and, in some sense, the duty of every man to make as much more money as he can, consistently with his obligations to himself, his family, and the world at large.

3. Every man must pay for whatever money he gets, and the price of wealth is very much greater than most men can afford to pay, and much greater than most men are willing to pay.

4. Money is good as a means to the accomplishment of worthy ends, but as itself an end, it is utterly unworthy of human effort, wherefore its pursuit, except as a means, must of necessity be debasing.

CHAPTER III.

THE CHOICE OF A BUSINESS.

THE IMPORTANCE OF CHOOSING WISELY.

An especially important part of every man's career is its beginning, upon which, in a greater degree than we are apt to think, depends the prosperity of the man throughout. The choice of a business determines the life of a man. It limits him on every hand, moulding him physically, intellectually, and even morally, sometimes; it determines how much and what kind of work he shall do; how much leisure he shall have; what books he may read; what his associations are to be; and in a hundred other ways affects his daily life to the end, and shapes his character far more certainly than even his previous education has done. It is, therefore, of the utmost importance that every one shall choose his business wisely, determining the question not, as is ordinarily done, upon caprice or under the influence of accidental circumstances, but upon a just estimate of his fitness for the business and the fitness of the business for him. So to choose is to avoid nearly half the errors which embitter human life. So to choose is to insure the spending of life profitably, worthily, and, for the most part, agreeably. Of an unwise choice comes failure, probably,—inefficiency and discontent, certainly. But to choose wisely, one must choose not carefully only, but intelligently, too. He must know himself as thoroughly as possible, and must govern his decision by correct principles, taking care that mere fancy shall have nothing whatever to do with it, and that no misapprehension of facts shall mislead him. A misstep here is fatal in most cases, and a source of ill always.

HOW TO CHOOSE A BUSINESS.

1. The first point to be considered, in the choice of a business, is your ability to earn a proper livelihood in its pursuit. If it does not give a reasonable promise of that, it is no fit business for you in any case. The laborer is worthy of his hire, and you have no right to withhold the hire, even though you be yourself the laborer in question. The world does not "owe you a living," as the phrase goes, but you owe it to the world to earn a living for yourself. You must live somehow, and have no right to live upon the product of other labor than your own.

2. It is necessary also to consider the question whether or not the business is likely to yield more than a living. Money in excess of one's actual needs is a powerful agent greatly increasing one's capacity for good work, and so this point is by no means to be neglected, though it is secondary in importance, to some others. Other things being equal, that business is best which will certainly yield a support and is likely to yield the largest surplus. But in order that other things shall be equal, several conditions must be satisfied.

3. As we have already seen, the world is entitled to your very best work, and in choosing between all the avocations which satisfy the first condition set down above, it is the imperative duty of every man to choose the one in following

which he is likely to do his best work. And by one's best work we do not mean work in the most dignified and so-called "respectable" employment he can follow, by any means, but the best work he can do of any kind. It is far better work to make particularly good horse shoes than to practice law or medicine only tolerably well. The man to whom nature has given a genius, or even a talent, for mechanics, positively wrongs his fellow-men when he chooses to devote himself to a business in which he is less able to excel. No man has a right to spoil a good blacksmith or carpenter for the sake of making an indifferent physician, or clergyman, or attorney. The world has need of best men in every walk of life, and we have no right to make a poor worker in one field out of a man who might have been a good worker in another. It is the duty of every man, in short, to ascertain, as nearly as possible, what talents he has,—for what he is best fitted,—what work he can do best, and to choose his employment accordingly.

Even if we put the claim of our fellow-men in the matter completely aside, and regard selfish interests only, we shall still find this in every way desirable. There is a joy in doing the thing for which we are fitted, that no man can know whose work is less truly in harmony with his nature. We enjoy doing the things that we can do well, while the imperfect doing of things in the doing of which we are conscious of a lack of the power to excel, is little less than a source of positive misery.

And a like result is reached if we measure the matter by a strictly pecuniary standard. The market is always overstocked with middling work of all sorts, while first rate work in every department of human effort, is always so scarce as to command high prices. Every newspaper editor, every merchant, every manufacturer, every employer of any sort, indeed, is constantly overwhelmed with applications from people who are capable of doing tolerably good work, while every employer knows that when he has need of a man capable of really first rate performance, he must search diligently for him, and pay him a high price when he is found. Now, the men who become capable of this sort of work, are those, and those only, who have devoted themselves to the business for which they are, by nature and education, especially fitted.

4. Your physical fitness for the business must, likewise, be considered. You have no more right to commit indirect than direct suicide. You owe it to yourself, to your family, present or prospective, and to the world, which has need of you, to live out your full measure of life, in health and in working condition, as far as the matter is within your control. If there be that in your constitution, or in the history of your family, which indicates a liability upon your part to particular classes of disease, you have no right to presume upon your present health, or upon chance good fortune, in choosing a business, the pursuit of which will add to the danger or diminish the safeguards against it.

5. In like manner, if you are likely at any time to be a married man, it becomes your duty, in choosing your avocation, to recognize the claims of wife and children upon your time and society. There are professions and trades, as everybody knows, which no married man can follow without unjustly depriving his family of the companionship which every man owes, as an imperative debt, to those who constitute his house-

hold. The man who is likely ever to marry has no more right to adopt one of these callings than he has to provide in any other way for the discomfort of the family which he intends to call about him.

These are the general considerations which affect and should govern the action of every man deciding what his calling shall be. Some points of hardly less importance remain to be mentioned. Most of them are included, expressly or by direct implication, in the foregoing statement of principles, but as they are often neglected in practice, it seems necessary to set them down here.

It is especially desirable that you shall *find your level.* A large percentage of life's failures, and many of life's miseries are due to people's persistent attempts to do things for which they are not fitted. A blunder of this kind at the outset is almost sure to embarrass one through life. One does not like to confess such a blunder; it is mortifying to give up what one has undertaken to do, on the ground that he is not qualified for the business, and there are hundreds of people who, by dint of favor shown, and by the unwise assistance of friends, manage to waste a life in the doing of poor work for poor pay, while they might be doing excellent work of some other sort, and living a life of personal independence and manliness. The trouble comes mostly from a mistaken notion of respectability. There is, even in our democratic country, a feeling that certain callings are in some way more respectable than others, and, unmanly as this feeling is, it misleads thousands to their ruin. In so far as it refers to the learned professions we may readily understand the prejudice, inasmuch as the successful pursuit of these, of necessity, implies the possession of both intellectual strength and culture, and these are matters worthily held in universal esteem; wherefore there is genuine dignity and honor in the pursuit of callings of this kind, provided the pursuit be successful. The dignity and honor belong not to the professions, but to the intellectual qualifications necessary to their successful following. There is no honor in unworthily doing anything. The practice of a profession without the necessary qualifications, only serves to emphasize their absence, and so the man who seeks honor by entering a profession for which he is unfit, secures contempt instead.

But the prejudice which holds certain callings more honorable or more respectable than others, does not confine itself by any means to the drawing of a line between those professions which presuppose culture, and those which do not. The idea seems a not uncommon one, that it is in some way more respectable to sell goods over a counter than to follow a mechanical pursuit, or, in general terms, that those avocations which may be followed in broadcloth are more dignified than those which may not. That these distinctions are not founded in reason becomes evident the moment one tries to trace them to their origin; but that they serve to mar many lives which might be useful ones, is unquestionably true. There must be salesmen in our dry goods stores, of course, but the demand is always greater for skilled than for unskilled labor, and the supply is nearly always in an inverse ratio. The mechanic has a technical culture,—a skill gained by years of patient study,—which the other has not, and the possession of such a culture is a just ground for honest pride, as well as a sure guaranty against poverty. In short, while all honest work is honorable and dignified, the skill of the mechanic, which is in itself culture, is a worthy subject of pride, and other things being equal, the mechanic is superior in fact to the unskilled worker. He can do a higher kind of work, and he is a more thoroughly educated man, in his fustian, than is his fellow in broadcloth, who, with no greater intellectual or educational endowments, lacks his technical knowledge.

There is still another mistake commonly made in this matter. It is not the erroneous notion of respectability alone which leads so many young men who ought to know a trade, into clerkships and salesmen's positions instead. There is a prevalent belief among young men that there are more and better chances for advancement in commerce than in mechanical pursuits. They mistake their own vague imaginings for well grounded hopes, and it is safe to say that half the young men who seek city clerkships look confidently for the coming of a time when they shall be merchants on their own account. They have heard of such things befalling others, and see no reason why it may not happen so with them. They ponder the stories of men who, beginning as office boys, have become chief clerks, junior partners, and ultimately even seniors in great houses, until these come to represent, in their eyes, the ordinary and probable course of affairs. They forget that success of this kind can come to but one man out of many thousands, and that when it does come it is the result of something more than mere chance. To a young man with capital in reserve, or with its equivalent in influence, or, still better, with extraordinary capacity, a clerkship may offer a reasonable prospect of ultimate advancement, but without one or another of these conditions, the chances are more than a thousand to one that he will never succeed in making more than a bare support for himself, while the overcrowded condition of the ranks in which he stands makes his position a precarious one always. The mechanic, on the other hand, brings a definite skill to bear upon the problem of money making. Only those who are similarly skilled can compete with him for employment. His skill is a positive capital, and his work is always productive. There are few "brilliant" opportunities open to him, though there are in reality quite as many as there are to the salesman or clerk; but he knows definitely how to do something which other men must have done, and which they cannot do for themselves, and if he be sober and industrious he is always sure of a support, while, with a wise economy, he may almost certainly accumulate a comfortable surplus in the end.

In general terms, it is important, in every case, that the worker shall know how to do some kind of work thoroughly well. In skill only is there any real safety from want. Even the possession of wealth is not half so sure a guaranty against poverty, and no man who is without a thorough knowledge of some business is ever safe. These are not new truths, but they need constant reiteration. Moreover, they are truer now and more important than ever before in our country's history. So long as this was a new country, with undeveloped resources on every hand, growing wild as it were, there were opportunities which no longer exist, for the easy and rapid accumulation of wealth. Almost any man of ordinarily good capacity might make money without definite skill, and while that was the case, knowledge of some business was far less important than it now is as a preparation for life. When every man who could turn his unskilled hand to any useful thing was sure to find work and wages, and when every purchase of a piece of land included the possible purchase of a coming city, there was less need than now of technical education. But the era of easy money getting is rapidly passing away. The work of developing our country's resources is only fairly begun, it is true, but it is so well begun that only skilled labor is wanted in its further accomplishment. The geography of our land is already definitely planned, and men of wealth have anticipated our growth by many decades in the purchase of land upon which towns are likely to grow. Skilled workers are to be had now where there were none a generation ago, and they inevitably crowd their unskilled fellows from the places which eagerly sought them heretofore. Unskilled brains and hands found abundant and remunerative employment when there were no others, but that day has gone by forever, and the young man who can offer the world nothing better than untrained ability, is sure now to be left standing idle in the market-place because no man has hired or is likely to hire him. The ease with which money has been made hitherto by people without definite skill, has bred a national vice in this regard, and nothing less than a generation or two of positive suffering will cure it effectually. But every man may avoid it for himself, and if this little book by warning its readers, shall persuade any considerable number of them to arm themselves against poverty by making themselves masters of some calling, it will serve its purpose well. I cannot emphasize too strongly the truth which I have sought here to inculcate. The indifference with which young men habitually allow themselves to drift listlessly into avocations for which they are by nature unfit; the confidence with which they trust chance to do for them that which they should do for themselves; and the blind recklessness with which they neglect to acquire a skill that may serve them in their life struggle, is simply appalling. If this little book might effectually warn its readers against so dangerous a course; if the author might hope to carry conviction to the half of them on this one point, he might fairly rest content. Learn a regular business, and learn it well! To teach that alone would be to tell young men "how to make a living."

PERSISTENCE IN BUSINESS.

Having learned a business it is almost always unwise, and sometimes it is even dangerous to change it either in whole or in part for any other calling. It is not at all probable that you will succeed better in a business which is new to you than in the one you understand, and so long as that yields you a support you cannot safely surrender it for something else. We have a national vice in this regard which is hardly less hurtful and dangerous than the one already alluded to, and it is a result of precisely the same causes. While unskilled workers were in demand, and unskilled work was profitable, it was safe enough and often advisable, to substitute one occupation for another, laboring to supply the demand of the day. The alteration which has taken place in the character of our country,—our growth from the condition of new settlements to that of populous states, has wrought a change in all this, and as it is now of paramount importance that every man shall regularly learn a business, so too it is only in the persistent pursuit of the business learned that there is now any safety. The temptation to change is often a very strong one, and it comes in many shapes. The danger lies chiefly, however, in the specious allurements of catch-penny callings. When one finds his own avocation a plodding one, yielding only its small regular wages, the temptation to change is strong. And when in such a case he is permitted to catch a glimpse of the occasional earnings of some follower of a precarious business, it becomes almost irresistible. In such a case it is well to remember, first, that *so much in a day* is not *so much every day;* and secondly, that for every man who succeeds in callings of this sort, at least ten fail utterly. The canvasser who makes fifty dollars in a day is certain to speak of the fact, but he is equally certain not to say anything of the many weary days whose work brought him nothing. Of the canvassers who fail entirely, we naturally hear nothing at all. The chances of success in callings of this general character (and these are the avocations which the people who change from one business to another commonly adopt) are very much smaller than the chances of failure. In truth not one person in a hundred has the qualifications necessary to win tolerable success in this kind of work. These qualifications are inherent, and not to be acquired in any way. Without them failure is simply inevitable, and most of us are in fact utterly destitute of them, wherefore a very large proportion of those who have tried business of this kind, have failed in the attempt.

The temptation to abandon one avocation for another is greatly increased by the false lights in which we see other people's work and other people's circumstances. Most men seem prosperous to their neighbors, who see only their mode of life, and their expenditures, knowing nothing of their toil or of the economy which they find it necessary to practise in private. So too, every man's work seems easier and more agreeable than our own, simply because we see it from the outside, knowing nothing of the drudgery incident to it, the difficulty of doing it or the poverty of its results as its doer knows them. Of our own work we tire now and then, and when we do we exaggerate its difficulty and the disagreeable things attending it. Its results are much smaller than we have hoped, perhaps, and we naturally assume that they are smaller than those attained by our neighbor. We draw unjust comparisons between his lot or his work and our own, knowing our own perfectly and his imperfectly. Now it is a well-ascertained fact that the profits of different handicrafts do not materially vary from one standard, and it is safe to say that there is no great difference between the net results of all the different avocations open to any one man. In other words, every man's money-getting power is limited by his character, his intellectual capacity, his education, and his capital. These enable him to follow any one of certain avocations, and his earnings will be substantially the same whether he adopt one or another of the callings thus open to him. What the result would be if he had a larger capital, or a better education, or greater capacity, and so were fitted for some business which he cannot follow at all as he is, it is not worth while to inquire. Such as he is, he is capable of making a certain amount of money, and he could hardly increase the amount if his business were other than it is. To change, therefore, from one of the businesses open to him to another which cannot pay better, is useless in any case, and, when the change is from a calling in which the man is an expert to one in which he is a mere tyro, it is sheer folly. And yet changes of this kind are made every day by men who seriously hope to better their condition in this way. Now and then one does benefit himself by such a change, and this fact serves to tempt others all the more strongly. But cases of this kind are rare exceptions to a well-nigh universal rule, and when they occur at all there is nearly always some factor involved which is not common to other cases at all. The man has some special fitness for the new undertaking; or was in some way specially unfitted for the old; or he is a man of more than ordinary versatility; or he has entered upon his new calling under peculiarly favorable auspices; or, as is sometimes the case, pure accident has come to his assistance. Whatever the cause of his success may be it is exceptional, and in no way affects the rule that it is always dangerous and often disastrous to change from one avocation to another.

If one is not succeeding satisfactorily in the business which he knows, he may safely assume that he will find it still more difficult to succeed in one which he does not know. And usually there is a discoverable cause for the imperfect success, and the remedy is commonly within reach. If you take pains to make yourself absolute master of your business, and give to it all the energy you have, success is certain. If you are doing listlessly that which needs to be done earnestly, you have only to rouse yourself to better performance. If you know imperfectly that which you should know perfectly, the shortest road to success is to stick to your work until you shall learn to do it with a master hand. It is not the best class of workmen in any calling who are out of employment, or whose work commands an inadequate wage. The fluctuations of business bear lightly upon these even while their less competent fellows are reduced to actual want. A reduction of force means always the discharge of the least efficient hands, and a reduction of wages strikes them first also. "There is room enough in the upper stories," said Mr. Webster, when he was reminded that the profession he had chosen was already overcrowded, and the remark holds good in all other avocations. To sum up briefly what has gone before, we say to every young man :

1. Select a calling for which you are fitted by nature, education and circumstance ;

2. Learn your business thoroughly, making yourself a master workman ;

3. Entertain no thought of changing from one avocation to another ;

4. Bring to bear upon your work all the energy and capacity you have ;

5. Do your work conscientiously, remembering that to do it ill is to defraud yourself, your family and the world ;

6. Respect yourself too much to hold your calling unworthy, bearing in mind the fact that that work is most honorable which is best done.

CHAPTER IV.

MARRIAGE AND MONEY.

THE VALUE AND THE COST OF A FAMILY.

CAN a young man, with his way to make, afford to marry? This is a question asked every day, and answered in various dogmatic ways, but it is rarely ever fairly examined, and as a consequence the answers given are rarely ever of value. Sentiment decides the point in most cases and there is as much of sentiment on one side as on the other. But there are well ascertained facts upon which to base a decision, and to these we ask attention. It is unquestionably true that no man should marry who is not able to support a family in tolerable comfort. But every man who knows a business thoroughly, and has reasonably good health, is able, in our country at least, to support a family, if he be right minded and master of himself. Without skill in some recognized calling, however, marriage is in the last degree dangerous, even to men with wealth already in possession. There is no certainty that one's wealth will remain with him. Skill is the only certain possession, the only thing which one cannot lose, and skill only is an adequate safeguard against ultimate poverty. The man who has skill to offer the world is sure of a market for his wares, and such a man need have no hesitation about marrying under proper conditions. And to such a man a family has a positive pecuniary value, much greater than the cost of its maintenance. The man of family has incentives, which no unmarried man can have, to constant exertion, to sobriety of life, to economy, to steadiness of purpose, to all those virtues, in short, which render business success certain and make business failure next to impossible. Married men, as a rule, are better workmen than single ones, in every branch of human exertion. They retain their situations longer. Their attention is less likely to be diverted from business to other things. Their earnings, in every kind of business, are usually greater than those of unmarried men; and their hold upon business is far surer than that of men who have only themselves to provide for. Against all these considerations must be set the cost of maintaining a family. But is there really any cost in the matter? Is there not rather a positive economy in marriage? As a rule, certainly, married men save more money than single men. They are not married men because they are better off than their fellows, but are better off because they are married men. The unmarried man has a hundred necessary expenses, which the married man escapes entirely. And the temptations which beset single men to spend money in unnecessary ways,—temptations of which the married man knows nothing,—are too well known to need mention. And the money thus unnecessarily spent is commonly sufficient to pay the entire expense of a family. The fact is that very few single men who must live from their work save anything at all out of their incomes, while nearly all married ones do. In other words, the majority of men find it more expensive to live single than to marry. As a rule, therefore, putting the matter on its lowest plane, we think it a wise economy to marry, provided the wife be a sensible person, accustomed to live in a style similar to that which her husband can afford.

MARRYING FOR MONEY.

Aside from the moral enormity involved, the very worst speculation in which any man can engage is that of marrying for money. Judged by purely economic laws, it is almost always dangerous, to say the least. Young women who inherit property are usually the daughters of wealthy men, and at any rate are accustomed to live in a style which the money or property they bring into the partnership will not suffice to maintain. In other words, the expense of maintaining such a wife is usually greater than the income her property can be made to yield, and, as a consequence, mercenary marriages of this kind are apt to result in an ultimate poverty which the wife does not know how to share with her husband, or how to remedy in the smallest degree. And the principle holds good in cases in which the marriage has not been a mercenary one at all, if the wife alone has brought money or property into the family. With the very best of purposes she does not know how to adapt herself to a mode of life less expensive than that which obtained in her father's house, and her inheritance alone is rarely ever sufficient for that.

This seems a homely treatment of such a subject, but the sad mistakes now and then resulting from ignorance or neglect of these facts, render it necessary in an unpretentious, practical manual like this.

THE EXTRAVAGANCE OF WIVES.

We hear a good deal of the extravagance of women, and of the ruin it works in men's affairs. Somebody once said that modern women are so extravagant in dress, and so helpless in other respects, that none but rich men can afford to marry them, and foolish people have been saying the same thing, or something like it, ever since. Every time a man fails in business people take a mental inventory of his wife's wardrobe, and cry out, "Poor fellow, he was ruined by her extravagance!" No account is taken of his club expenses, or his unnecessary restaurant bills, or his fast horses, or the vanity that prompted him to buy a bigger and finer house than he needed, and to furnish it in a style which he could not afford. Nothing is said of his dress coats made by some Monsieur Snip who charges extra prices because he writes himself "Artist Tailor" on his gilded sign. The man may have gambled his money away, or he may have lost it in reckless stock speculation for all any body knows to the contrary, while his wife, whom he has deluded into the belief that he is rich, has dressed and lived only as his seeming circumstances justified her in doing, doing it too for his sake, chiefly, that he might not be ashamed to introduce her as his wife,—that his home might be pleasant,—that he might feel free to have his friends as guests, and sometimes for the sake of the business advantages resulting from a graceful hospitality. Or if she has been as extravagant as he, the fault is usually his, so long as the fact remains that a proper husband may practically control a proper wife in matters of this kind, without sacrificing any part of her affection or in any way marring her happiness. It is true enough that women are not commonly taught the value of money or the principles of economy as they should be; but for the most part they are not fools. They have commonly no more stomach for beggary than men have. The ruin of their husbands is their ruin also. Poverty and changed circumstances fall far more heavily on them than upon their partners in life. The man goes to his business and spends half his life outside his home. He has respite every day from the discomforts of a cold hearthstone. The woman lives at home, and suffers. To her poverty is ever present. Its pains are her constant companions, and on her shoulders fall all the hardest duties incident to it. It is she who must pinch and save in ungraceful ways. Of the burden of the ruin she must bear the larger share. And knowing all this, women do not willingly work ruin in their husbands' affairs. That they bring it about sometimes, is true enough, but they do so unwittingly in nearly all cases, and it is clearly the fault of the man that they know not what they do. In short it is not true that the sin of extravagance lies always at the woman's door, and when it does it is nearly always the fault of the man, he being the cause, she only the agent of the ill. Men's personal expenses are not commonly so evident to others as women's are. A man spends money in a hundred ways of which his neighbors know nothing, while the extravagance of a woman is almost certain to be ostentatious. Indulgence is his object, display hers, and so his sins are covered while hers advertise themselves. And even that which seems to be her extravagance, is often his. The new carpet may have been bought at his behest, that he might seem prosperous in the eyes of his friends and guests, but the wife is blamed if a catastrophe happens to reveal the fact that the purchase was an unwise one.

In any case the man has an ultimate power to control matters, which, if he be a wise man, he will exercise, and if necessary, he may do so too, in nearly every case, without doing or seeming to do any arbitrary act whatever. As we have already seen, the wife is even more deeply interested than the husband, in the financial prosperity of the family. Upon her, too, depends, in a larger degree, the execution of whatever plans of economy the case may make necessary. She is commonly better able than he to manage such things, and she has better opportunities. It only remains to impress upon her the necessity of economy to secure its practice. She will not willingly work her own and her household's ruin, and if she be permitted to understand just what degree of economy prudence requires her to practice, she will practice it. Every married woman knows that she may be left a widow, with children to maintain, and nearly every married woman is anxious to prepare for such a contingency by the accumulation of means while the means are to be had. But every woman also wants to live as comfortably as she can. If she be right-minded she desires to make her home a specially attractive place not for her own sake only or even chiefly, but for the sake of her family. To reconcile these two desires with each other,—to accomplish the one end with the least possible sacrifice of the other, is the problem which every married woman has to solve, and most of them honestly and earnestly endeavor to solve it satisfactorily. But how are they to do so if they are left, as they commonly are, in ignorance of the factors with which they have to work? That they are left in ignorance, nay that they are positively misled in very many cases, is undeniably true, and the fault in every such case is with the man who misleads or neglects to enlighten them as to the facts. Women are neither idiots nor children. They may not know much of the laws of finance, but they do know that if they spend more money than their husbands make, the end will be financial ruin. But what is a woman to do, who, naturally and properly anxious to live genteelly and comfortably, is vaguely told that she must economize, but is at the same time left in ignorance of the amount of money she may legitimately spend? Economy means one thing or another, according to circumstances. That which would be almost a niggardly economy on the part of one man, would be outrageous extravagance in another. The term is a relative one always, and means just nothing at all to one who knows nothing of the income to which it relates. To tell the wife to economize, without telling her also what the husband's income is, is to talk to her in a language of which she does not know the alphabet. And when to such folly is added the injustice of misleading her as to the extent of your resources, by your own self-indulgence, or even by indulgence shown to her, she is certainly not to blame if her conception of the economy necessary shall prove wholly inadequate. She has a right, and it is her positive duty to dress and live as well as you can fairly afford. This duty is quite as imperative as the duty of practising economy, and the two are entirely consistent with each other. That she may do both, she must know what you can and what you cannot afford. If you leave her to guess the factors of the problem, you have only yourself to blame when she involves you in her failure to solve it. No sane man would think of entrusting the management of an important branch of his business to a partner, and keeping that partner in ignorance of the facts underlying the business itself, even if he could find a partner willing to be kept in such ignorance. But in an important sense every wife is her husband's business partner. She not only keeps the expense account, but governs it also, and she can govern it wisely only when she knows upon what it rests. Having a duty to do in the matter, she has a right to the information necessary to its proper performance.

THE ADVANTAGES OF DOMESTIC PARTNERSHIPS.

And while it is the right of the wife to share in her husband's business sufficiently at least to be able to manage her part of it wisely and well, it is clearly the interest of the husband to make her his advisory partner even to a much greater extent if possible. The duties and responsibilities implied in such a position give healthful occupation to her mind for one thing.

The wife who is fully informed of her husband's business affairs; who knows what his means and his necessities are; who is able to decide for herself from facts known to her, what measure of economy is prudent, will naturally plan and execute a system of saving which will accomplish its purpose with the least possible friction, and with the smallest sacrifice of comfort to her family. Such a woman has many incentives to economy which her less fully enlightened sister can never have. She is constantly able to adjust the family expenses to the family purse, and as she guesses at nothing, she is not likely to make serious mistakes. Above all, she becomes as much interested as he in the success of a business upon which both depend for prosperity, and of the progress of which she is fully informed, and there are a thousand ways in which she may and will contribute materially to its successful prosecution. She is an excellent adviser in very many cases, and a conservative force always, and every business man knows how sorely conservatism is needed in most men's affairs. When for any reason the business becomes less profitable than usual, the well-informed wife sees the necessity for domestic retrenchment, long before most men would think it necessary to point the matter out. The wife who from the very first is informed of her husband's circumstances, has her attention directed constantly to the common object of securing present prosperity and future competence, and this is a great gain in every case. The steady pursuit of such a purpose, by man and wife acting together, is pretty sure to end in its accomplishment. In short, the young man with his way to make in the world cannot do a better thing than take his wife into confidential partnership from the beginning.

THE DIFFICULTIES IN THE WAY.

There is one principal difficulty and several minor ones in the way of doing this. The principal difficulty is that people do not begin aright. The young married man, acting under a variety of motives, usually conceals from his wife the exact extent of his means, and in his anxiety to gratify her wishes as well as to spare her from pecuniary care, he directly deceives her, however unintentionally, as to his ability to afford expenditure. In this way it happens frequently that serious embarrassment results from the unwise expenditure, in a few months, of the money which should have supported the family for a year or two. Besides, having begun wrong, there is necessarily some degree of mortification to be incurred when a change in their mode of life becomes necessary, and, anxious to avoid this, the husband commonly postpones the change as long as possible, even running into debt sometimes and laying a burden upon his own and his wife's shoulders which must be borne for years. And so a misstep in the start makes the journey a halting one throughout. There are so many mistakes of this kind made, and their consequences are so very serious, that we cannot lay too much stress upon the necessity of beginning right. When two people marry, it is presumable that they wish and intend to be as prosperous and happy as they can. Their interests are precisely identical. Upon the wise administration of their affairs, both at home and in business, depends, in a large measure, the success of their efforts to live happily. Knowing all this, common sense ought to teach them the necessity of a clear understanding at the very outset. They must work together with common means for the accomplishment of a common end, and there can be nothing more absurd than an attempt to do this while one of the joint managers,—and that the one upon whom chiefly falls the duty of maintaining a just ratio between expenses and income,—is kept ignorant of the state of the family exchequer. The only sensible course,—the only course, indeed, in which there is even tolerable safety, is for the man who provides the means, to enlighten the woman who controls expenditures, as to the exact resources at their joint command. The folly and cowardice which prompt a course of concealment and deception, are unworthy a man, even if they were not shamefully unjust also. It seems strange that any man should be ashamed of his own lack of wealth,—and that one should blush to own it to his wife would be inconceivable if it were not every day manifest.

CHAPTER V.

HOW TO LIVE ON YOUR INCOME.

MR. MICAWBER'S RULE.

THERE was a deal of wisdom in Mr. Micawber's dictum, that if a man has twenty pounds a year for his income and spends nineteen pounds nineteen shillings and sixpence, he will be happy, but that if he spends twenty pounds one, he will be miserable. We all recognize the truth of this, as heartily as Mr. Micawber did,—and a good many of us imitate his utter neglect to practice the precept which he was so fond of laying down for the guidance of others. We have need of very little arithmetic to teach us that if we spend more money than we get we shall be ruined. It is a self-evident proposition that one must live within his income, whatever it may be, if he would prosper, and yet it is by no means an uncommon thing for people to spend every year more money than they earn. The people who do this do not covet ruin by any means. On the contrary, they are for the most part the very people who are least able to endure the poverty they bring upon themselves, and their fault of over expenditure is due largely to the fact that they are incapable of practising even a part of the self-denial which the ultimate poverty that must come from their present recklessness, will impose upon them of necessity. They are usually those who most earnestly desire to accumulate money for the sake of its comfort-giving power, and the trouble is that they cannot wait till they have earned the comforts they seek before indulging in them. They are sanguine people, commonly, who have a gift of seeing a large prosperity ahead, and who are apt to anticipate it in their mode of living. They live upon the money they intend to make, rather than upon that which is already made. I happen to know one such man whose annual income during the past ten or twelve years has never been less than four thousand dollars, and yet he has gone deeper and deeper into debt with each succeeding year, simply because each year has brought with it the hope that the next would prove greatly more profitable than any of its predecessors.

He has never once relinquished his purpose to accumulate a moderate sum of profitably invested money, upon which to retire from active business, and that he might have done so before this time is evident, if he had been content to govern each year's expenditures by the year's earnings, rather than by next year's promise. His case is an extreme one, perhaps, but the principle involved is very common. Almost every man who lives beyond his means intends to live within them. His failure to do so is due, in most cases, to self-delusion of some sort, and rarely if ever to a deliberate purpose or even to a conscious recklessness of consequences.

WHAT IS YOUR INCOME?

In view of these facts, which are everywhere evident, it is of the utmost importance that there should be something more than a vague purpose to adapt the living to the means of living. And the first thing to be done is to ascertain what your income is; not what it is to be; still less what you hope it may be, but what it is. There must be no uncertainty of any sort about the matter. Vague ideas, approximate estimates, are fatal in all business matters. The merchant is not content to know the details of his business approximately. He takes care to learn the *exact* amount of his expenses, the *exact* cost of goods, the *exact* extent of his sales, and exactitude is certainly not less essential in dealing with the problem of how to keep one's expenditures within one's means.

But even this is not all. You must not only know what your income is, but also what you can certainly keep it in the future. A salary which may be reduced or cut off entirely next week, or next month, or next year, is no safe measure of your ability to spend. To a certain degree your income, whatever its nature and its source may be, must be the measure of your expense, but if its continuance be uncertain you cannot wisely expend as large a share of it as you might of an equal income of a more certainly permanent sort. Possible periods of reduced earnings or of no earnings at all must be admitted as factors in the problem, and it is the average to which these may reduce your earnings that should be your standard. If you can keep within that average you are safe, but not otherwise. And should your precautions prove in the end to have been unnecessary, the only result will be a larger sum saved and a speedier accomplishment of the purpose with which you sat out.

HOW TO KEEP WITHIN THE AVERAGE.

Having ascertained what amount of money you can certainly count upon as your income, it will be comparatively easy to keep your expenditures within that limit. You will know at any rate how much you can afford to spend, and as over-expenditure results in a great degree from the lack of precisely this knowledge, you will at least be much safer with than without it. You will know what is the nineteen pounds nineteen shillings and sixpence which you may spend with safety.

But in fixing the limit of your expenses a little below that of your income, it is necessary to remember that this must be not the minimum, not the average even, but the maximum of your outgo; and as next week or next month may bring an unforeseen necessity for extraordinary expense, your only safety lies in providing in advance for such contingencies. It is never safe to trust to future economy to repair the waste and restore the disturbed equilibrium.

By living now below the limit you have set, you can provide against the failure which may otherwise come of some unexpected circumstance; and while such provision is always possible, it is not always possible to reduce an average after it has been swelled beyond the limits you have assigned it. If you find thirty dollars a week to be the amount you can afford to spend throughout the year, it is the part of prudence to spend only twenty-five now, so that when sickness or other accident shall compel you to exceed the amount for a time, your safe average may not be transcended in the end. Neglect to do this has made saving impossible to hundreds of people, and we hear every day of families reduced to starvation by reason of some unexpected and unprovided-for sickness, on the part of the producing member.

WHEN TO SAVE.

I once knew a man whose rule in life it was to spend all the money he could get and to stretch his credit also to its utmost limit, and he justified this on the ground that unexpended money and unused credit were of no account in the sum of life's enjoyments. And there may be other such men, but without doubt they are exceptions to the rule. Most people distinctly intend to save something out of their incomes, and, more than that, most people intend to save a good deal in the end. That so many of them fail to do it, is due, in this country at least, to the fact that they neglect some one of the conditions essential to the accomplishment of their purpose. And a point on which very many stumble is the one now under consideration. They do not know *when* to save. They intend to save largely as soon as the immediate pressure of present wants shall be relieved. Next week, next month, they will certainly save, but just now it is impossible. On nothing else do so many slip. The trouble is that it always seems easier to economize after a while than now. Next week's necessities do not assert themselves as those of the present do. We do not discover all of them in advance, and those which we do see seem far less pressing than they will when we shall come to them. And so we exaggerate our ability to save hereafter, while we neglect to save now, at the same time cultivating a fatal habit of self-indulgence which is likely to prove one of the greatest difficulties in our way. There is just one time to economize, and that time is *Now*. If you would make sure of the end you seek, you must save something to-day and every day, never once offsetting to-day's neglect with to-morrow's possible performance. In this matter of saving, more than in almost any other, procrastination is fatal. To save requires deliberate self-denial. He who puts away any portion of his income must of necessity deny himself an exactly equivalent portion of the things which that income is capable of buying, and there are few people indeed whose incomes are so large that this may be done without a direct and earnest effort. Now it is not only true that the spirit of self-indulgence which prompts the gratification of to-day's desires and the postponement of self-denial to another time, will give a like prompting when that other time shall come ; but it is equally true, and even more important, that habit in these matters is very strong ; self-indulgence breeds a habit of self-indulgence which cannot easily be conquered; and on the other hand, a habit of saving is born only of the practice of saving.

WHERE TO SAVE.

A very common trouble in this matter of putting away a part of one's earnings for future use is the failure to appreciate the value of small things, or rather the failure to appreciate the saving worth, if I may so put it, of the very smallness and valuelessness of little things. In other words, we are apt to regard the pennies or fractional notes in our pockets as too small to be worth saving. We intend to save, but rarely ever find it convenient to spare a five or ten dollar bank note from our pocket-books, and deeming smaller savings hardly worth attention, we end by putting away nothing because we cannot put away a good deal, or, more truly, because we cannot put money away in what we deem worthy amounts. Now the fact is that nearly all the saving that is done at all is done in small sums. The deposits in savings banks amount to many millions, but they consist almost wholly of very little sums of money; and so well is this principle recognized in institutions of that sort that they all make it a rule not only to accept but especially to encourage small deposits, many of them taking as little as a single dime, willingly, in spite of the fact that every deposit makes necessary an amount of clerical work which the dime would hardly pay for, even if it were given to the institution outright. As a rule, therefore, the place to begin saving is in little things. The pennies which lie loose in one's pocket should be the first objects of attention, and after these, fractional currency must be considered. No one ever realizes, until he has subjected the matter to the test of experiment, how much money passes through his hands annually in very small pieces. I happened to be present one day, when a man of very limited means was discussing the possibility, for he was in no doubt whatever as to the desirability, of insuring his life. He urged the fact that with all the economy he knew how to practice, he never yet had been able to count fifty dollars as spare money; he insisted that it required absolutely all the money he could make in his business, to meet the actual wants of his family, and without doubt he had always found it so. The agent replied, however, with a remark that startled all who heard it "A policy of five thousand dollars will only cost you *ten cents*, and you can save that by wearing your boots a week longer than you commonly do."

"*Ten cents?* What do you mean? The premium according to your own statement is a hundred and nine dollars a year."

"That is very true," replied the agent, "and yet you will only have to save ten cents, or at any rate you need never be conscious of saving more than that, to meet the payments. I'll explain what I mean. Take a child's safe,—it will only cost you ten cents, and whenever a ten-cent note comes to you in making change, slip it into the safe. If two or three come at once and from the same person, put only one in. I'll advance the first payment myself, and when the second falls due we'll open the safe. If there isn't enough in it to pay me back, after paying the second year's premium, I'll stand the loss. And if you miss the money so put away, you needn't continue the policy."

The proposition was both novel and startling, and in accepting it the man, who was a merchant in a country place, warned his friend that he should hold him to his promise. A year later I went with the agent to see the safe opened. Instead of one there were several of the little tin receptacles, each stuffed full of fractional currency; but the merchant was confident that the aggregate could not be more than fifty dollars.

"But it is fifty dollars saved," he said, "for truly I haven't missed it anywhere."

When the boxes were opened they were found to contain just two thousand eight hundred and seventy-four bits of green paper, or two hundred and eighty-seven dollars and forty cents,—considerably more than enough to pay the two annual premiums.

The anecdote is a homely one, but it serves to point a

moral. It shows the value of small sums, and their capacity to make a considerable aggregate when systematically saved.

HOW TO ECONOMIZE.

But this is only one side, and the less important side of the matter. As small sums are more important than we are accustomed to think, and are more easily and more surely saved than large ones, so, on the other hand, it is in small things that we may, with the least effort, practice economy. Having discovered the necessity of cutting down expenses, you are pretty sure to cast about you for some place of saving. You mentally run over your current expenditures in the hope that you may find some considerable item which may be reduced or cut off entirely. And the hope is nearly always disappointed, for the reason that in matters of any considerable cost, most people are already practising quite as sharp an economy as they conveniently can. Everybody wonders, now and then, where all his money goes, but not one man in a hundred ever satisfies himself on the subject. Not one man in a hundred indulges unnecessarily in things which must be paid for in a lump. When called upon to pay out a sum of money which is considerable if measured by the standard of our ability to pay, we are sure to scrutinize pretty sharply the desirableness of the thing paid for and our ability to do without it. In short, we are not apt to be extravagant in large matters, and in point of fact there is very little room for economy in such things, in most men's affairs. It is the little things that we buy thoughtlessly in which we are extravagant, and it is these things which we may do without, either in whole or in part, without serious inconvenience. It is by cutting off expenditure for these that we may save, and the aggregate of the cost of these is always much greater than their purchaser imagines, especially with people who live in cities. An intelligent, thrifty mechanic once told me that he had bought and paid for a comfortable home, merely by reducing his own personal expenses in three particulars. He blacked his own boots, walked to and from his work instead of riding in the street cars, and brought his lunch from home instead of taking it at a restaurant. His saving amounted to about fifty cents a day,—a mere trifle,—but in ten or twelve years it enabled him to buy a good home without denying himself any real comfort, and without imposing any burden whatever on his family. He had been able to see no other place of saving, and probably there was no other in his case; but most of us have a variety of expenses which might as well be stopped as continued, and so most of us may do a good deal more than he did by the judicious application of an economic pruning-knife.

And there is still another reason why it is easier to save in small things than in matters of more importance. It is much easier to deny ourselves small comforts and small luxuries than large ones. There is a magnified desirability in large things which it is difficult to resist, and to reduce expenses by denying ourselves the things of considerable cost to which we are accustomed, requires a good deal more of moral courage than ordinary people are possessed of, while he must be very weak, indeed, who cannot deny himself little comforts and luxuries of temporary importance only, or of no importance at all, for the sake of permanently bettering his financial condition.

PURCHASES BY WHOLESALE.

There is, within the reach of nearly all the people who are likely to read a book of this kind, a simple and easy way of saving about one-third the cost of all family supplies,—namely, by buying everything at wholesale. It is very convenient to give daily orders at the grocer's for such things as are immediately needed, knowing that they will be promptly delivered at one's residence, but the convenience is one for which purchasers must pay a round price. The grocer does not pay rent and keep a horse and a man " merely for the fun of the thing," as I once heard a business man phrase it, and it is a pleasant little fiction that he delivers goods " in any part of the city, free of charge." He does nothing of the sort, for the simple reason that he has no interest in doing it, and cannot afford to do it. He makes no specific charge for delivering goods, it is true, but he charges for it nevertheless, adding the amount to his prices. There is very little profit, we are told, in keeping a retail grocery, and the statement is doubtless true, and yet any one may satisfy himself by experiment, that he can buy his groceries at wholesale for at least one-third less than the retailer charges him, provided he buys a stock of several articles at once. Sometimes the saving is considerably greater even than this, but this much is certain in any case, and such a saving makes a very pleasant little account to contemplate, in a savings bank, at semi-annually compounding interest.

But this is not all. The saving of the difference between wholesale and retail prices is not the only advantage gained by any means. As we have already said, one scrutinizes the want he is providing for, if it must be paid for in considerable sums, as he does not where its cost is met by the daily expenditure of small amounts, and when one buys his supplies at wholesale he realizes the necessity of using them judiciously, as he never can in any other case. Again, when the supplies are to be bought the money must be provided, and to provide it one must often economize closely in other ways, which is of itself an advantage. The people who do not buy at wholesale are very often the people who can least afford to purchase otherwise. They buy at retail because they never have money enough in hand to make a wholesale purchase possible, and if they could be persuaded to change their habit, the effort to save something for the purpose would teach them the lesson they most need,—namely, *how* to economize.

CONCERNING LITTLE BILLS.

Another convenience which you cannot afford, if you have need to save anything, is that of keeping an open account with your butcher, your baker, or anybody else. In the first place, money is always worth interest, and no tradesman has enough of it to enable him to let it out for nothing, else he would not be a tradesman at all. He who buys his goods on credit, therefore, must, in one way or another, pay for the indulgence. He has the use of another man's money and must pay interest on it. And this he does, whether the item appears in his weekly or monthly or quarterly bill or not. Interest is charged in every case, even though the tradesman himself be unconscious of the fact, as he very often is. His experience has taught him what percentage he must add to the cost of his goods to make a living profit, and in determining this, experience has duly included interest upon outstanding bills as one of the factors in the problem.

A second reason for avoiding bills is found in the fact that you are well-nigh certain to buy a good deal more when you buy upon credit than when you pay cash. The tradesmen all know this, and it is for precisely this reason that they take the risk incident to time sales. The extra purchases which customers buying upon credit are sure to make, constitute the inducement to that mode of doing business. When you must pay for everything you buy at the time of buying, you are constantly and forcibly impressed with the costliness of the articles purchased, as you never can be if the payment be postponed, and so the cash buyer scrutinizes the wants to be supplied, much more surely and much more sharply than his neighbor who purchases upon credit is apt to do. The amount of cash you have,—if you owe nothing,—is an exact measure of your ability to purchase; and as the whole science of economy and thrift consists of buying somewhat less than you can afford, it will be seen at a glance that even without the other considerations urged, this one fact should be an all-sufficient argument against the practice of "running bills."

You have no right, in justice to yourself and your family, to buy anything you cannot afford; and if you have not the money with which to pay for anything, you cannot afford to buy it. It is, in the last degree, unwise to charge upon a future, which is likely to have burdens enough of its own to bear, any responsibility for the present, and especially for present extravagance, and every purchase you make beyond your present ability to pay, is an extravagant one.

The necessity of paying cash for every article bought, cannot be too strongly insisted upon. Saving is well-nigh impossible where this rule is violated. Its enforcement may require a pretty sharp self-denial, but that is the very best possible evidence that its enforcement is needed, and, in the end, the cash buyer is sure to live better than he possibly could under any other rule.

I hardly need explain that I have reference here only to the purchase of articles for consumption. It is no part of my purpose to discuss the system of credit which obtains in the commercial world, and which is governed by laws of its own.

THE PARALYSIS OF DEBT.

Another objection to the practice of making bills, and the one most frequently urged, lies in the fact that debt paralyzes one, saps his energies, destroys his vitality, and so lessens his power to make money and weakens his purpose to save it. And all this is quite as true of harassing bills as of the larger debts which overwhelm one. Indeed it is, in many cases, truer. Large debts may be dealt with in ways which are not available in the case of small ones. Commercial failure, if it be accompanied by no dishonesty, does not bring disgrace with it; and debts which cannot be paid may be disposed of by compromise with creditors or by process of bankruptcy, leaving the debtor free to begin again. It is not so with petty bills; failure to pay these promptly brings disgrace and sore annoyance. There is a conviction on the part of those who know the facts, and, worse than all, a consciousness on the part of the delinquent debtor, that his purchases have been in some sense fraudulent. And even when one does not fail to meet his bills, it costs a good deal, in the way of anxiety, to provide for them. They come in at unseasonable times, and their payment overthrows plans which might otherwise have been carried into effect. Sometimes it serves to show the debtor that money which he had thought saved is, after all, spent, and the discouragement which this produces is, by no means, a strong incentive to renewed exertions. In short, it is not too much too say that small bills are a sort of dry rot upon one's finances, which very few people can successfully withstand. There is no good reason for making them in any case, and they are dangerous always. That men who make them do prosper now and then in spite of their evil influence, is true enough, and so do men recover from small-pox and yellow fever sometimes, but we do not dread those scourges the less on that account. No man who can afford to have open accounts against him at the grocer's, the butcher's, the dry-goods man's, and the baker's, has any occasion to have them, while those who feel the need of such indulgence are the very people who cannot afford it at all.

THE EXPENSIVENESS OF SHAM.

When one reflects upon the costliness of the shams to which nearly everybody resorts, and sees what sad work they make now and then, it seems a pity that custom has not decreed that a statement of every man's exact financial condition shall be written up over his door. No observant person can doubt that absolutely unnecessary expenditures, which add literally nothing to comfort, constitute a considerable item in the sum of well-nigh everybody's outgo. I refer now not to the insane recklessness, pictured in story so frequently, which prompts people once rich to pretend to be so still, and so to sink themselves both morally and financially into the mire, but of the every-day shamming of sensible people, unconscious of a desire to appear better off than they are. When you lay aside your last winter's overcoat because, while it is whole and comfortable, it looks a trifle shabby, and buy a new one with money which ought to have gone into the savings bank, you are shamming, and it is costing you a good deal, too. The desire to dress as well as your fellows is worthy enough, but if you really cannot afford to do so—which is to say that to do so you must use money which ought to be put away for other purposes—you are a very foolish and a very cowardly person to do it at all. It is more manly, as well as wiser, to dress less genteelly than your fellows, to live in a cheaper house than they, and to practice economies they never dream of practising, than to wrap yourself in lies as you do whenever you put on clothes which you cannot afford, or in any other way spend more than your income justifies you in spending, merely for the sake of conforming to the customs of those about you. And yet there are very few people, indeed, who do not, in one way or another, act falsehoods of this kind every day. How many men are there with moral courage enough to refrain from all the expenses which they cannot afford! How many are there who never feel that they pay a higher rent than they ought; that their tailor's bills are inconveniently large; that their net surplus, after paying all, is smaller than it should be! It is true that in the great majority of cases men do not blame themselves for these results, because it is much easier and less humiliating to make their wives and families the scapegoats for their own sins of extravagance. It is easier to sigh and say, "Well, well, a family is an expensive luxury," than honestly to own that one has been a moral coward and spent more money than he could afford, because he has been afraid that somebody might suspect him of being poorer than he is. So common is this sort of extravagance that nine workingmen in ten, and sometimes even the tenth one also, have it in their power to make an entirely satisfactory saving every year, merely by putting a stop to all those expenses which are incurred for the sake of appearances only, and which bring no real good in return. I know a printer who, after several years of hard struggling, found himself as poor as when he began life, and, having this fact pressed upon his attention, he resolutely put the plan suggested into practice. From that day to this, he tells me, he has lived in greater comfort than he ever did before, and a constantly growing account at the savings bank has made him in a measure independent of fortune. He had never been consciously extravagant. On the contrary, he had pinched in a hundred ways that his earnings might support his family, but, like the rest of us, he had allowed the practice of others to regulate his mode of living, and, as is usually the case, that mode of living was more expensive than he could afford. A very wealthy gentleman, whose history I happen to know, began life with absolutely nothing. He left home a mere boy, owning, as he puts it, one pair of tow linen trowsers, one tow linen shirt, and one tow linen suspender. His father, a shrewd old Scotchman, gave him this piece of parting advice :

"Money that you haven't earned is not yours, and will do you no good. Remember that, and remember that everybody around you spends more money than he can afford." The boy was not long in learning what this last statement meant, and now that he is a rich man, with scores of boys and young men in his service, he often tells them that the secret of prosperity consists in remembering that nearly everybody is a spendthrift.

PERSONAL EXPENSES.

It is especially important, in every effort to economize, that you shall keep your own personal expenses within proper limits. As a rule, household expenses cannot very well be reduced to any considerable extent, except in the ways already pointed out, simply because, as a rule, they do not greatly exceed the measure of the household needs. The family must be fed, clothed, housed, and warmed, and beyond the attention we have urged, to the proper and economical purchase of the supplies needed for this purpose, it is not often that economy can save much from the aggregate of expenditures in this direction. But the personal expenses of nearly every man greatly exceed the measure of necessity. Even those of us who imagine that we spend nearly nothing on ourselves do in reality waste a good deal of money that might be saved with little effort and no actual inconvenience. The waste is in small sums, insignificant in themselves, but amounting in the aggregate to a good deal. A large share of the money thus expended is used in supplying artificial or imaginary wants—wants created by the artificiality of our lives or by the constant sight of articles which, if we saw not, we should never think of wanting. The very fact that the vendors of these things, from the great merchants to the keepers of peanut stands, find it profitable to display their wares to the public gaze at considerable cost to themselves, is proof enough of the unreality of the wants they supply; and if further evidence be needed, one has only to keep an account of the things he buys in town which he could not get at all if he lived in the country.

THE HABIT OF SELF CONTROL.

To deny oneself indulgences of this sort is to save in the aggregate a good deal more than any one who has never given the matter attention is apt to think, and there is a value in such self-denial of even greater worth than the money it enables one to save. It cultivates a habit of self-control, than which nothing can be more essential to success of any kind. Indeed, it is the absence of this habit which, more than any other one thing, makes saving impossible to many people. It is because we do not know how to control ourselves and to deny ourselves that so many of us fail, not only to save money, but to accomplish any other end we set before us. The most eminently and uniformly successful business man I ever knew makes it a rule of his life to deny himself something which he wants, every day. In his youth he acquired the habit of smoking for the sole purpose of abandoning it, so that he might always have a craving appetite to keep in subject.on, confident that the habit of self-control which this would give him would be of great advantage to him; and that it has been, there can be no doubt whatever. Its effects can be traced all through his vast business operations. Temptations to launch out into dangerous speculation bring no danger to a man so constantly in the habit of subjecting all his wishes and impulses to the control of reason. The habit gives him, too, a singular mastery over others as well as himself, and to the remotest corners of his wide-reaching business, his control extends almost without an effort. It is not in making money alone that he has succeeded. He has undertaken many other things in his time, and has never yet known a failure. His mastery of himself makes him master of others, and almost equally master of circumstances. He has organized success and reduced its factors to an unfailing formula, of which self-control is the principal element. It is precisely this habit of subjecting impulse to judgment-informed will that we call persistency, in estimating character; and persistency is the condition of all worthy achievement. Without it, genius itself leads only to brilliant failure, and with it mediocrity often wins the reputation which we are accustomed to think belongs only to genius. In investigating the great problem of gravitation, Sir Isaac Newton made a number of the most ingenious and brilliant guesses. If he had contented himself with these he would not have solved his problem, but he would have won a world-wide fame as a genius, nevertheless. And if he had been less truly master of himself than he was, there can be no doubt that he would have cherished and defended these brilliant conjectures to the last. As it was, he weighed and tested each, scrutinizing it as closely as if it had been the guess of a rival of whom he was jealous. Regardless of its brilliancy, its ingenuity, its capacity to reflect credit upon himself; regardless, also, of toil and delay; regardless of everything but truth, he examined each of his hypotheses and rejected each in its turn until by the method of exclusion he sifted error out and left only the grain of truth with which the world has linked his name. It was by self-control, persistency of character, that he finally reached the end he sought, and this homely habit contributed a good deal more than his genius did to the building of his enduring fame. And it is precisely the same in all other walks of life. Massena and Macdonald were not altogether the most gifted soldiers Napoleon had with him in the field, and yet they succeeded in accomplishing things which none of their fellow-marshals could have achieved. At Essling, where Napoleon was beaten, the successful withdrawal of his army depended upon the power of Massena to hold his position for a considerable time. The task was so difficult of accomplishment that even the imperious will of Napoleon shrank from demanding it of his marshal. Instead of an order, therefore, he sent a request that Marshal Massena should hold his position for two hours. The indomitable marshal had been battling ceaselessly for more than forty hours already, was exhausted, sick, half dead, and could barely sit erect and look with bloodshot eyes at the messenger as he delivered the request of Napoleon. But Massena was absolute master of Massena, and his reply was: "Tell the Emperor I will hold out two hours—six—twenty-four—as long as may be necessary for the safety of the army." And he did what he promised.

At Wagram, Macdonald was charged with the task of piercing the Austrian centre, and when he found the position of the enemy apparently an impregnable one, he might well have been pardoned for retiring before impossibilities. He was too truly his own master, however, to admit that any desirable end was to him impossible of accomplishment; and so, leaving a black swath of dead men in his rear, he marched steadily onward until, with a loss of ten men out of every eleven in his corps, he finally pierced the line and gave victory to the French army. It was the habit of self-control which did it all, and this truth is taught on every page of history. He must be a poor reader of biography who has failed to discover that the universal key to success is mastery of self. It was this which enabled Washington, with a handful of well-nigh mutinous men in an impoverished country, to hold out for seven long years against well-disciplined, well-equipped, well-fed, and well-armed foes, and ultimately to convert failure itself into success. It was this which made Pitt the most renowned statesman of his time or of any time. It was this which made Franklin a phenomenon of success in everything he undertook, from money-making in a little shop to diplomacy and statesmanship. It is this which has enabled the Astors, Stewarts, Girards and Coopers of the country to build colossal fortunes from nothing; and it is this which must underlie every genuine success, large or small, achieved in any walk of life. If you feel that you are not master of yourself, that your impulses, your hopes, your fears, your longings, your antipathies are not under the dominion of your judgment and your will, be sure that there are holes in your armor, and that you are in no fit condition to engage in the battle of life. The defect is a dangerous one, which may prove fatal also, but it is not incurable. Man is so wholly the creature of habit that he may make himself, to a great extent, what it pleases him to be. To acquire the habit of doing a thing, you have only to do it constantly and persistently. To form the habit of self-control, you must control yourself. Cross your impulses at every opportunity. Deny yourself coveted indulgences. Spur yourself to continued exertion when you weary of a task, and, if your case be a bad one, persist in undertaking and accomplishing distasteful things. And it is a mistake to suppose that a habit of this sort brings unhappiness with it. On the contrary, it is the key to happiness as to everything else. There is no real or at least no permanent pleasure in momentary indulgences; there is no pleasure in weakness; there is none certainly in failure. It is conscious strength which is genuinely happy, and well-earned success brings a joy with it which nothing else can produce. There is a pleasure in conscious mastery of self which alone is more than sufficient to repay one for the labor expended in acquiring it, and no man is so truly free as he who knows himself his own only master.*

* As I send these pages to the press, I discover that some of the historical illustrations used in this chapter have been employed for a nearly identical purpose by Mr. E. P. Whipple in his admirable volume of essays which bears the title "Character and Characteristic Men" in Osgood's collected edition of his works. Whether this is merely a coincidence, or whether I have unconsciously borrowed his ideas, I am wholly unable to determine; but an author who scatters the best things so lavishly as Mr. Whipple does whenever he writes must expect that his poorer neighbors will borrow them now and then. And I am much more deeply concerned for the practical usefulness of this little manual than for its originality or its literary excellence.

CHAPTER VI.

WHAT TO DO WITH SAVINGS.

GENERAL PRINCIPLES.

EVERY man who saves anything, whether much or little is apt to find himself at some loss to know what to do with his savings. If he seek advice, he will find opinions as various as are the people who give them, and in the end he must decide for himself. To do so wisely, it is necessary to keep certain general principles in view, and while these will not always point in the same direction, attention to them will at least serve to prevent serious mistakes.

KEEPING MONEY AT WORK.

In the first place, one should never allow any part of his money or property to lie idle. The capacity of money to work and to earn wages is well enough known, doubtless, but it certainly is not as generally recognized and acted upon as it should be, particularly in the matter of small sums. The interest on a few dollars is apt to seem too small a thing to deserve attention, but the fallacy of this becomes evident if we reflect that, at simple interest of six per cent., money doubles itself while one's children are growing to manhood, and if the interest be promptly reinvested, or added to principal, twice a year, as is done in the savings banks, it will multiply itself by three within the nonage of one's children. Now the smaller your savings are, the greater is your need of the earnings they are capable of making and even if you have some other investment in view,—some investment to be made as soon as a sufficient sum for the purpose shall be accumulated,—it is unwise to allow your weekly savings to lie idle meanwhile. However brief the time, and however small the interest may be, your money should be made to work while it waits. For this purpose, and particularly in the case of small savings, the savings banks offer altogether the best and most convenient facilities. One can deposit very small sums there at any time, and so long as they remain they earn semi-annual, compound interest, which is to say that they double themselves in about twelve years, with a proportionate earning for shorter periods. Here certainly is a matter deserving attention, and it would seem incredible, if we did not know it to be a fact, that men who can never afford to be idle for a single day, allow their money to do nothing when it might be earning something all the time.

SAFETY OF INVESTMENTS.

A second point to be considered in determining what one's investments shall be is *Safety*. So far as small weekly or monthly savings are concerned there is little choice of course. The only way in which they can commonly be made to earn anything is by deposit in a savings bank, and these institutions, particularly the older ones, afford every guaranty of safety. Money placed with them is greatly more secure than if it were kept at home or about its owner's person. In the matter of making small sums immediately productive, therefore, there is but one course to pursue. Deposit them promptly in every case. But with larger amounts a variety of investments become possible, and with this possibility come temptation and danger. The owner of a few hundreds or a few thousands of dollars, is pretty sure to have pressed upon him various plans by which his cash can be made to pay much larger returns than the six or seven per cent. of ordinary loans. There are state, county, school, township and railroad bonds to be had in every broker's shop, which pay or promise to pay, directly or indirectly, ten, twelve, or fifteen per cent., and when one feels the necessity of making his money work, he is very apt also to desire that it shall earn good wages, and the temptation to invest it in securities of the sort described is greatly increased by the plausible showing which the vendors of the securities are always prepared to make for them. Now it is undeniable that in some cases money has been made by the purchase of these bonds below their par value, but it is nevertheless true that such purchases are never safe and never can be. A county or corporation so badly off for money that it must borrow it at eight or ten per cent. interest, affords no very great security for ultimate payment. And when its credit is so bad that in addition to promising high rates of interest it must sell its bonds for less than their face, which is too often the case, the insecurity of the investment ought to be apparent upon its face. It should be remembered that there is always a vast amount of money in New York *earnestly seeking investment.* It belongs to people skilled in discovering the real value of securities, and its owners are abundantly able to take some risk. Under these circumstances it is not likely that any really well-secured bonds, bearing seven, eight or ten per cent. interest, will ever lack purchasers at or above par, and when high interest bonds are hawked upon the street at less than their face, we may be very sure that they are not safe, whatever an interested broker or a subsidized religious newspaper may choose to say in their favor.

And, aside from this, it is a universal truth that high interest means poor security. It is with corporate bodies as with individuals. Those that are able to owe and to pay their debts have no occasion to raise money by paying for it more than it is worth. They may have need to borrow, but they can always borrow at the market rate.

All this seems evident enough, and yet it is lost sight of every day, and the results are sometimes very disastrous. The trouble is that there is nothing in the world so delusive as financial sophistry. From the time that credit first entered into commercial transactions until now, men have been busily endeavoring to create wealth out of nothing, and now and then theorists imagine that they have discovered how to accomplish it. It is so easy to delude not one's neighbors only but oneself, as well with sophistical financial reasoning, that the danger is present wherever credit enters into business transactions, however honest and well-meaning the authors of the mischief may be. Paper money is in itself so easy a thing to create that its use often engenders the idea that wealth itself may be ground out of a paper-mill. In this country this delusive idea has of late years gained a much firmer foothold than many people think, and under the stimulus given to speculation by the use of our depreciated and irredeemable paper, schemes of all sorts have been set on foot, most of them seeming safe and honest enough, but all of them designed in one way or another to create wealth out of nothing, by means of bonds and stocks and mortgages. We have been building railroads and doing other very costly things which we cannot pay for, simply because we do not own money enough. We have expended more than we have had, without knowing it. Under the influence of an unreal money, vast enterprises were projected all over the country, the aggregate cost of which was greatly more than we could possibly pay. This, as we now know, was the fact, but until the fall of 1873 it was not evident to most people. Sophistry covered it up and nothing seemed plainer than our ability to spend all these millions which we did not have. The projectors of a railroad organized themselves into a company, and placed their stock on the market. Cities, towns and counties, likely to be benefited by the road, bought most of it, giving in payment their bonds, bearing heavy rates of interest. Selling these, usually at a considerable discount, the directors were able to make some progress in the work of building the road. With a partially built road as security, the company could issue its bonds, on first and second mortgages, and these, bearing a high rate of interest, could be sold at something less than their face, bringing money enough into the company's treasury to carry forward the work. All this looked well enough, on its face, except to those cautious people who saw that the aggregate of these various securities was actually greater than the aggregate amount of means likely to be available for their redemption, and so, wearing a fair enough face, securities of an utterly unsafe sort have been sold to tens of thousands of poor people anxious to get high rates of interest. In the end a large part of these obligations must be repudiated, by one process or another. A railroad built on a double system of credit, and running through a country which can never give it business enough to pay interest on its indebtedness, must of very necessity fail somewhere. It may pay gold interest for a time, by means of still further borrowing, but sooner or later its creditors must lose, for the simple reason that the road and its business are worth less than the amount for which they stand as security.

It is impossible, of course, for me to lay down in a little manual like this, any rule by which to distinguish safe from unsafe investments, except the general one that high interest means poor security, and the universal one that wealth cannot be created out of nothing, by any process whatever, however ingenious and plausible the plans for accomplishing such things may seem. We live in a time of bubbles,—many of which seem solid enough,—and it is of bubbles especially, that the owner of moderate amounts of cash has need to beware. He should remember that it is the business of the men who blow these bubbles to make them seem very real and solid affairs, and their skill in doing this is so great that they are themselves deceived, oftentimes, by the plausibility of their own sophistries. The banker who, some years ago, undertook to show that "a great national debt is a great national blessing," was so infatuated with his own imagined discovery of means by which to create wealth out of nothing, that he unhesitatingly put his own private fortune at stake in the next great bubble he had occasion to blow, and the courts are just now busy settling his affairs and gathering up the fragments of the ruin. When he announced and undertook to prove his absurd proposition regarding a national debt, that very fact ought to have warned everybody against his schemes, proving as it did, that the great banker was a dangerously wild theorist, however honestly and earnestly he might believe in his own devices for using non-existent wealth in the prosecution of costly enterprises. The warning was unheeded, however, and thousands of people have lost their life's earnings as a consequence.

In warning readers against the investment of savings in bubble securities, I refer not so much to the schemes and traps of dishonest tricksters as to the well-meant efforts of theorists who honestly believe they have discovered how to accomplish financial impossibilities, and whose schemes wear so fair a face as to deceive even skilled men of business. And while it is impossible so to define bubbles of this sort that they may be readily distinguished from more solidly founded enterprises, a sketch of the most famous of all financial theorists, with an outline of his career, may serve to show in some measure how dangerously plausible utterly unsound theories of finance may be made, and how even "the very elect" of hard-headed business men, may be deceived, when tempted by a promise of enormous gain. I find the story so well told in Chambers' Miscellany (Tract No. 126), that instead of re-writing, I copy here a portion of the excellent text of that admirable work.

THE STORY OF JOHN LAW'S LIFE.

Among the inhabitants of Edinburgh, during the time when the national enthusiasm for the Darien scheme was at its height, was a youth, John Law, commonly called John Law of Lauriston. He was born at Edinburgh in 1671, his father being a rich goldsmith and banker in that city, who had purchased the lands of Randleston and Lauriston in the parish of Cramond. His father dying in 1684, left him his heir; and young Law, during the period of his education in Edinburgh, distinguished himself greatly by his mathematical abilities, and especially by his acquaintance with all matters relating to banking and finance, for which his father's profession had inspired him with a natural taste. On entering into manhood, he appeared to abandon these pursuits, and to be ambitious only of shining in society, for which he had the qualifications of a handsome person, and a great fund of wit and generous animal spirits. Removing to London, he plunged into all the gayeties of the metropolis, and became one of the most successful gamblers of the fashionable clubs, being dignified, according to the custom in such cases, with the name of Beau Law. In 1694 he became involved in a quarrel with Beau Wilson, a noted personage of that period; and a duel ensuing, in which Wilson was killed, Law was tried, found guilty of murder, and sentenced to death. On a representation of the case to the crown, a free pardon was granted to the offender; but a brother of the deceased having lodged an appeal against the pardon, he was detained in prison, and the issue might have proved serious, had he not made his escape to the continent. On the 7th of January, 1695, an advertisement appeared in the *London Gazette*, offering a reward for his apprehension, but without effect. After spending a few years on the continent, during which he employed himself in adding to his previous stock of knowledge by personal observations in various countries, directed especially to the trade and manufactures which they carried on, and the systems of banking established in them, he returned to Edinburgh at the time when the mind of the nation was universally agitated by the Darien Scheme. Here Law found himself in his element; and he was one of the many projectors who busied themselves in inventing schemes for enabling the kingdom to bear up against the crash which followed the ruin of the colony at Darien.. Fortunately, none of his projects were listened to, greatly owing to the active opposition of Patterson, who to the end of his life fought for the principle on which he had based the Bank of England—namely, that paper money must be *payable in coin on demand.*

Law, therefore, finding that he was still exposed to danger on account of the death of Wilson, again betook himself to the continent, travelling through Holland, Belgium, Italy, and France, and everywhere gaining the reputation of being one of the ablest, best-informed, and most agreeable gentlemen, and one of the most successful gamblers ever known. Although spending most of his time as a gambler and speculator for his own private behoof—an occupation to which no discredit was then attached—Law's mind was still busy with those great subjects of national economy, for which he considered himself to be, and for which he really was, gifted with an extraordinary natural capacity. Meeting on familiar terms with the highest personages in every city or state which he happened to visit, he was accustomed to throw out his ideas about finance in his conversation; and in this way his fame as a theorist extended itself far and wide. In France especially, owing to his intimacy with the Duke of Orleans, his reputation was high. It is even said that it was proposed to Louis XIV. by Desmarets, his finance minister, to adopt a plan offered by Law for remedying the disorders of the finances of the kingdom; but that Louis, on being informed that the schemer was a Protestant, and not a Catholic, refused to have anything to do with him. Law, indeed, appears to have been considered as a person somewhat too dangerous to be allowed to remain long in a country; he was banished both from Genoa and Turin. Proposing his scheme of a paper currency to the Duke of Savoy, afterwards King of Sardinia, that prince answered:

'No, Mr. Law; I am by far too poor a potentate to be ruined; but, if I know the French, they are exactly the people with whom you will succeed.'

Law eventually came to the same conclusion; and in 1714 he removed to Paris, and fixed his residence in the Place Vendome, mingling again with the best society.

In 1715, Louis XIV. died, and the Duke of Orleans became regent during the minority of Louis XV. The revenues of the kingdom were in a state of frightful confusion, and there seemed to be no way of avoiding a national bankruptcy. The national debt amounted to 3,111,000,000 livres, bearing an interest of 86,000,000 livres. The only means of paying this interest was out of the excess of the revenue over the expenditure; but as this amounted only to the small sum of 9,000-000 livres, it was insufficient to meet the demands of the state creditors. By means of strenuous exertions, the regent contrived to reduce the national debt to 2,000,000,000 livres, and the interest to 80,000,000; further reduction was considered impossible, and the state was believed to be on the brink of ruin. (The *livre* was almost of the same value as the later franc, 25 of which are equivalent to a pound sterling; 100 livres were thus about equal to £4.) At this crisis the Scottish theorist came forward, and offered to relieve France from her difficulties. In various ways, both by writings and by actual interviews with the regent, he pressed his great idea—the establishment of a paper currency. Gold, silver, copper, or any other kind of coin, he said, which a nation may agree to use, are not real wealth; they are only signs or representatives of real wealth, and derive their value from public confidence. It does not matter, therefore, what the kind of coinage be which a nation agrees to use; a paper coinage or a leather coinage is as good as a metallic one. A metallic coinage does not constitute real riches, but is valuable only because the public choose to consider it valuable; and if the public will only do the same with paper notes, then paper notes will be on an equality with gold or silver coin. What is a louis d'or but a bank note, only made of gold; or a crown but a bank note, only made of silver? It does not signify, therefore, what a nation chooses to consider money, be it even oyster shells; for such will serve as a sign or representative of real wealth the same as a piece of metal.

This reasoning is correct only so far. Gold certainly does not constitute real wealth: it is not food, clothing, or the means of shelter, all which are so many items of real wealth; but it possesses a greater intrinsic value than paper, and therefore is not so completely at the mercy of public opinion. Apart altogether from its fictitious value as a coin, gold is a useful and a precious metal, for which there is a demand in the arts;

and the cost of obtaining it from the bowels of the earth, and refining it, being great, every little piece of gold is, as it were, a condensation of a quantity of real wealth; paper, on the other hand, is a valuable commodity likewise; but the cost of its production being less, it really has less intrinsic value, and is more dependent upon public opinion. Paper can be procured as abundantly as we choose; but there is a limit to the production of gold. Gold and silver are dear substances in themselves; paper is a very cheap substance. The value of a metallic currency, therefore, is not so liable to fluctuation as one entirely of paper.

Not laying due stress upon these considerations, and others of a more profound nature, Law maintained that in a country 'where there exists no circulating medium but gold and silver, its riches may be greatly augmented by the introduction of paper money'—a proposition true only so long as what is issued represents real wealth, and does not go beyond the legitimate demands of the circulation. What Law proposed to the regent was to establish a national bank, which should issue notes on the basis of landed property and of the royal revenues—the bank to be conducted in the King's name, but subject to the control of commissioners appointed by the States-General. The project having been considered by the council of finances, it was decided, on the 2d of May, 1716, that 'the present conjuncture was not favorable for such an undertaking.' Law, however, obtained leave to set up a private bank, under the name of 'Law & Company,' the funds to be furnished by himself, and such as chose to become shareholders. The stock was to consist of twelve thousand shares, at one thousand crowns (£250) each, and was therefore to amount in all, to £300,000. The bank was not to be allowed to borrow money, nor to engage in any kind of commerce. But the most peculiar feature of the establishment, and that which gave it favor in the eyes of the public, was that its notes were to be payable at sight, *in specie of the same weight and fineness as the money in circulation at the period of their issue.* This was a novelty; for since the year 1689, the currency had been subject to constant alterations—the value of the livre to-day being perhaps not much more than half what it was yesterday. On this account, as well as from the quickness and punctuality of the payments, and the orders given to the officers of the revenue in all parts of the kingdom to receive the paper of Law's bank, without discount, in payment of taxes, the notes of the bank in a short time rose to great repute, and were by many preferred to specie, in so much that they soon came to pass current for one per cent. more than the coin itself. The most beneficial effects were thereby produced on the industry and trade of the nation; the taxes and royal revenues being, by means of the notes, remitted to the capital at little expense, and without draining the provinces of specie. Foreigners, who had hitherto been very cautious in dealing with the French, now began to interest themselves deeply in this new bank; so that the balance of exchange with England and Holland soon rose to the rate of four and five per cent. in favor of Paris. The bank subsisted in high credit, to the no small profit of the proprietors, till the close of the year 1718, when the Duke of Orleans, observing the uncommon advantages resulting from the establishment, resolved to take it into his Majesty's hands, as at first proposed.

Law and the other shareholders apparently disliked this proposal, but they were obliged to yield; and on the 4th of December, 1718, the bank was declared to be a Royal Bank, to be administered thenceforward in the King's name, His Majesty having reimbursed the former company, and become answerable for the notes issued by them. Law was appointed director-general of this Royal Bank, and branches were immediately established at Lyons, Rochelle, Tours, Amiens, and Orleans. Various alterations in the mode of management were also introduced.

If the bank had continued to perform no other functions than those which are usually understood to belong to a bank, there is every probability that its establishment would have been a considerable advantage to the nation. But in the course of three years after its establishment, the bank had incorporated with itself many other schemes of various characters, so that, instead of continuing a mere bank, it became a gigantic commercial company. In 1717, an institution was established under the directorship of Mr. Law, called the 'Company of the West,' or, more commonly, the Mississippi Company; to which a grant was made of the whole of that tract of land on the American Continent through which the river Mississippi flows—this tract at the time being French property. The stock consisted of 200,000 shares at 500 livres each. On the 4th of September, 1718, the farm of tobacco was made over to this company for a consideration; three months afterwards it acquired the charter and property of the Senegal company; and in May, 1719, it obtained from the regent a monopoly of trade with the East Indies, China, and the South Seas, on condition of paying the debts of the East India Company, then dissolved. Thus enlarged, the company abandoned the name of the Company of the West, and assumed that of the 'Company of the Indies,' at the same time creating 50,000 additional shares at an increased price. Nor was this all. In July, 1719, the Mint was made over to the Company of the Indies for a sum of money; in August following, the farming of the whole taxes of the nation was purchased by the company; and the privilege of receiving other branches of the revenue quickly followed—so that before the end of the year 1719, the Company of the Indies had incorporated within itself nearly all the commercial enterprise of the nation. Law was thus the director and manager of two great national institutions—the Royal Bank, and the colossal trading company called the Company of the Indies. In February, 1720, these two were united; and Law, the founder of both, became the most powerful man in France. Between the date of the incorporation of the two concerns and the first of May, 1720, the bank ordered a fresh issue of notes to the amount of 1,696,400,000 livres—making the total quantity issued amount to the enormous sum of 2,696,400,000 livres.

The end of the year 1719 and the beginning of the year 1720 was a period of wild infatuation. Such was the confidence entertained in the system of Law, and such the avidity for wealth, that the shares of the Company of the Indies rose with unexampled rapidity, every one taking it for granted that the speediest way to realize a prodigious fortune was to become a shareholder to as large an amount as possible in the India Company. The frenzy extended to all ranks and classes.

'Clergy and laity, peers and plebeians, statesmen, princes, nay, even ladies who had, or could procure money for that purpose, turned stock-jobbers, outbidding each other.' The shares soon rose to 5000 livres each. Prudent shareholders now began to sell out, and with the enormous fortunes which they had realized, to purchase houses and estates. The sight of opulence thus rapidly acquired increased the popular delirium, each man saying to himself: 'Why may not I realize a fortune, and purchase houses and estates, too?' The state creditors, likewise, being paid in bank-notes, such a quantity of paper was thrown into circulation that it could be disposed of in no other way than by the purchase of East India stock; and the competition of these purchasers against each other increased the price of shares still more rapidly. In November, 1719, they were sold at 10,000 livres each, or at twenty times their original price.

Innumerable anecdotes are told illustrative of the eagerness of all classes to become shareholders in the company, of the intense anxiety which prevailed, arising from every fluctuation in the value of shares, and of the strange vicissitudes of fortune which were brought about during the frenzy. The street in which the stock-jobbers met at first was the Rue de Quinquempoix; and the crowds which used daily to assemble there were so great that accidents were constantly occurring. The occupiers of this street reaped a golden harvest from the general excitement by letting their houses to the speculators. Houses whose rent was 800 livres a year were let at 6000 or 10,000 livres a month; and even single apartments were let for a pistole (16s.) a day. A cobbler earned 200 livres a day by allowing ladies and gentlemen to sit in his stall, furnishing them with chairs and writing materials; nay, one hump-backed man is mentioned as having acquired a fortune of 150,000 livres by allowing the jobbers in the street to use his hump as a writing-desk. M. Chirac, physician to the Duke of Orleans, was on his way to visit a lady, one of his patients, when he was informed that the price of shares was falling. His mind was so engrossed with the news, that, while feeling the lady's pulse, he exclaimed in agony: 'Oh it falls, it falls continually!' And the lady, alarmed, began to shriek, till he reassured her by telling her it was the Mississippi shares, and not her pulse, he referred to. No one was able to withstand the infatuation. Two of the ablest scholars and most learned men in France, the Abbe Tenasson and M. de la Mothe, were lamenting together the madness of the nation, and congratulating themselves on the fact that, being scholars, they had escaped the contagion. A few days after, the Abbe, pushing through the crowd at the Rue de Quinquempoix, met M. de la Mothe pushing through it also—both having come to bargain in the stocks. In the whole court only five persons refrained from speculating, and those who did so were regarded as cowards or fools.

The Rue de Quinquempoix being found too narrow for the immense crowds who congregated daily for the purpose of speculating in the India stock, the traffic was transferred to the Place Vendome. In a short time, however, this open space was also found inconvenient; and Law, at an enormous price, purchased the Hotel de Soissons, in whose gardens pavilions were erected for the accommodation of the public. Here the business was daily carried on.

Mr. Law, as the author and dispenser of all the wealth for which the nation was struggling, became, beyond comparison, the principal personage in the kingdom. The levee of the Regent was forsaken; and princes, dukes, peers, bishops, and judges, crowded the retinue of the Scottish projector. His ante-chambers were constantly full of ladies waiting for an interview, that they might prevail on Mr. Law to sell them a portion of stock. Troubled by such numbers of applicants, Law conducted himself with the utmost haughtiness, and would keep a peer of the realm waiting five or six hours before admitting him to an interview. Enormous bribes were given to his servants on condition, merely, that they should announce the name of the person waiting. It was to the French aristocracy that Mr. Law behaved in this haughty way; to his own countrymen, and to persons coming on ordinary errands, he appears to have been exceedingly affable. 'The Earl of Hay, afterwards Duke of Argyle, going to wait upon Mr. Law by appointment, found the ante-chambers filled with many of the highest quality of France; but being, by special orders, admitted into his private apartments, beheld the great man writing what, from the number and rank of those left to wait his leisure, he naturally concluded to be dispatches of the utmost consequence. Upon mentioning these surmises to his old friend, it was with no small surprise his lordship learned that he was only writing to his gardener, at Lauriston, to plant cabbages in a particular spot! After this important epistle was concluded, he desired the Earl to play a game at piquet, at which they continued for a good while, till at length the great man thought proper to give orders for the admission of his humble supplicants.' Many amusing anecdotes are told of the stratagems fallen upon by the ladies to procure an interview with Mr. Law. A Madame de Boucher, being extremely anxious to possess some India stock, made every effort to procure an invitation to meet Mr. Law at dinner at the house of Madame de Simiani, where she knew he was to be present; but, as it was known Mr. Law did not wish to see her, Madame de Simiani could not comply with her friend's request. Resolved, nevertheless, to gain her point, the lady ordered her carriage to be driven past the house; and when exactly opposite to it she gave the alarm of fire. The guests, Mr. Law included, rushed into the street. The lady jumped out of her carriage and was hurrying up to him but, perceiving her design, he took to his heels and escaped. Another lady gave orders to her coachman to be on the watch for Mr. Law in the streets, and the moment he saw him close at hand, to overturn the carriage. It was several days before the longed-for opportunity arrived; and the lady, being the first to perceive the approach of the great man, called out to the coachman: 'Upset me now, you rascal!—upset me now!' The man did as he was ordered; Law flew to the lady's relief, and had her conveyed in the Hotel de Soissons. Here the lady confessed her trick, and Law, as a reward for her ingenuity, was obliged to enter her name as a purchaser of stock.

So sudden and rapid was the rise of the price of shares, that enormous fortunes were made in the course of a few days. Many instances are recorded of persons in the lowest ranks of life suddenly realizing immense wealth. One night, at the opera, all eyes were attracted by a lady in a magnificent dress, sitting in a very conspicuous position; and no one could make out who she was, till a young lady whispered to her mother: 'Why it is our cook, Mary!' and it proved to be so; Mary had been speculating and become rich. A footman had speculated so successfully as to be able to set up a carriage of his own; but when entering it for the first time, the force of habit was so strong that he mounted into his accustomed place behind—excusing himself, as he jumped to the ground again, by saying he was trying how many lacqueys would have room to stand on the board. Mr. Law's coachman had made such a fortune, that he asked his discharge, which Mr. Law gave him, on condition that, before going, he should supply him with another coachman as good as himself. The man brought two coachmen next day, recommended both as excellent drivers, and asked his master to choose one as he meant to engage the other himself. Another speculator finding himself a rich man, gave orders to a coach-maker for a magnificent new berlin, leaving 4000 livres as a deposit. The coach-maker inquiring what arms were to be put on the carriage, 'Oh, the finest—the finest, by all means!' said the fortunate man. One Brignand, a baker's son, having acquired an enormous fortune, and wishing to have a superb service of plate, went into a goldsmith's shop and purchased the whole collection of articles exposed for sale at 400,000 livres.

Up to this time Law's system had produced nothing but the most wonderful outward prosperity; and when the state of the nation was compared with what it had been at the death of Louis XIV., it appeared that the man to whose exertions the change was owing could be nothing less than a demigod.

Money circulated in profusion, people in the lowest ranks indulged in luxuries previously unattainable, and the price of commodities rose without any injury to the people. The ell of cloth which had sold for fifteen livres now sold for fifty; and the pound of coffee rose from fifty sous to eighteen livres. Wages rose correspondingly. In the course of three months, the silversmiths of Paris had received orders for, and manufactured above £7,000,000 worth of plate. Paris was crowded with foreign visitors, who had come to speculate in the stocks. No fewer than 305,000 strangers are said to have been living in Paris in November 1719, and many of these were obliged to live in granaries and lofts, there not being sufficient house accommodation for them all. The promenaders in the street were clothed in velvet and gold; and the winter of 1719–20, was more brilliant than the finest summer ever seen before.

Law was now the idol of the country, and the enthusiasm in his favor was greatly increased by his making a public profession of the Roman Catholic religion in December 1719. The only obstacle to his admission to political dignity being thus removed, he was declared comptroller-general of the finances, in January 1720, a situation equivalent to that of prime minister of France. About the same time the Academy of Sciences elected him an honorary member. Honors and applause were showered upon him; and, among the rest, the poets, 'a venal gang,' vied with each other in preparing compliments for the savior of France. It was to be expected that the man who was enriching others by his scheme would grow wealthy himself; accordingly, Law is known to have realized an enormous fortune. He had purchased fifteen or sixteen large estates, together with houses and mansions, amounting altogether to the value of 7,000,000 livres. It is to be remarked, however, as a proof of Law's good faith and his confidence in his own system, that he invested all his money in landed property in France, which, in the event of a crash, would be completely lost to him, and did not send any sums out of the country, as he might easily have done. It appears, indeed, that he wished to purchase the estate of Errol, in Perthshire; but the bargain was never concluded. His generosity was equal to his wealth. On the occasion of his professing himself a Roman Catholic, he gave 500,000 livres to assist in completing the church of St. Roch; he distributed another sum of 500,000 livres among the English at St. Germain-en-Laye, whose pensions had been suppressed; and his private liberalities was constant and munificent. Lauded and spoken of all over Europe, Scotland began to be proud of him, and contrived to let it be known that it was she who had given birth to such a genius. The city of Edinburgh transmitted him its freedom in a gold box. English and Scottish noblemen boasted of being acquainted with Mr. Law, and it is even said George II., then Prince of Wales, condescended to dabble secretly in the Mississippi stock.

The bubble, however, was already full blown. The credit of the bank and of the India company was at its height in the months of November and December, 1719, and January, 1720, when shares in the company was selling at 10,000 livres each. Such was the abundance of money in the bank, that it offered to lend sums of any amount, on proper security, at an interest of only two per cent. Now, however, a drain of specie from the bank began to be discernible. Numbers of persons possessed of stock in the company—either foreseeing disaster, or haunted with a vague suspicion that so prosperous a state of things could not last long—began to sell out, and convert their shares into gold and silver, and other precious commodities, which they either hoarded up, or sent secretly out of the country. The Prince de Conti, offended at being refused a quantity of fresh shares, for which he petitioned, sent to the bank to demand specie for so enormous a mass of notes that three wagons were required to carry the money from the bank to his house. Vernesobre de Laurien, a Prussian, whom Mr. Law had appointed a cashier in the bank, remitted nearly 40,000,000 livres to foreign countries, and then disappeared. Various stock jobbers remitted hundreds of thousands of louis d'ors to England. These examples were imitated by others —for nothing is more contagious than fear—and in a short time 500,000,000 livres in specie were sent out of France.

To put a stop to this run upon the bank, which, from the immense quantity of notes in circulation, would be ruinous, a series of edicts were issued by the regent in February and March, 1720. By these edicts payments in specie were restricted to small sums (not exceeding 100 livres in gold and 10 livres in silver), while at the same time efforts were made to secure a preference for paper over specie, by declaring the value of the former to be invariable, while that of the latter fluctuated. People were also prohibited from converting their wealth into gold and silver plate without a royal license, the demand for plate having been one of the principal means of withdrawing the precious metals from circulation. The exertions thus made were for some time effectual; and numbers seeing notes passing current at 5 or 10 per cent. above specie, hastened to convert all the specie in their possession into paper. There is, however, in the minds of men at such a time a natural preference for the metals over paper; and accordingly it was found that many were busy in secretly hoarding up gold and silver, and cautiously disposing of their paper in anticipation of the coming crash. Fresh edicts of a more stringent and arbitrary character were issued; one forbidding the use of specie altogether in payment, another forbidding any person to have in his possession more than 500 livres of coin, under the penalty of having the sum confiscated, and the payment of a fine in addition.

In an instant—so suddenly, in fact, that it is impossible to trace the steps of the process—the nation, which had been glorying in its good fortune, was struck with dismay and despair. The use of specie had been prohibited; but this could not restore confidence in Law's paper, and nobody would accept it willingly. It was felt universally that Law's scheme had been *a bubble*, and that it had now burst. Complaints and execrations arose everywhere against Law, the regent, and all who had been concerned in originating the project. To crown Law's misery, many of the influential men of France, who had all along hated him and been envious of his honor and reputation, but who had been restrained from showing their ill-will by his success, now attacked him in the presence of the regent and accused him of plotting the ruin of France. The regent even, who had hitherto been his intimate friend and in compliance with whose solicitations Law had adopted some of his most questionable measures, turned against him.

All efforts to arrest the progress of the panic were in vain. In consequence of the decree ordering all payments to be made in paper, a fresh issue of notes had taken place; and in May, 1720, the notes issued amounted to 2,600,000,000 livres, while the quantity of specie in the kingdom was estimated at 1,300,000,000, or only half as much. To equalize the paper with the specie there were two plans; either to double the value of the specie, or to halve the value of the paper. Law advised the former, as being a thing to which the people were quite accustomed; but his advice was overruled; and on the 21st of May an edict was published reducing the value of the paper by a gradual process till it should be exactly half its present value—a note for 10,000 livres passing current for only 5000, and so on. This reduction of the value of the bank notes was, it will be remembered, a violation of the original constitution of Law's bank, according to which it was faithfully promised that the notes should never fluctuate in value, but be always equal to a given quantity of specie of given fineness. If paper had been disliked before, the promulgation of this edict made matters a thousand times worse. Bank notes were regarded as waste paper; and a person might have starved with 100,000 livres of paper money in his pocket.

On the 27th of May the bank stopped payment in specie; and on the same day Law was dismissed from his office as minister of finance. There were riotings and mobbings in the streets, and the various quarters of Paris were occupied by troops to prevent an insurrection from bursting out. Law's life was several times in danger; the regent was under the necessity of giving him a detachment to guard his person, as he drove through the streets; and at length, not safe in his own house, he took refuge in the Palais-Royal.

D'Aguesseau, who had been dismissed from the Ministry in 1718 on account of his opposition to Law's projects, was now recalled; and by his advice a decree was passed on the 1st of June, repealing the decree forbidding the amassing of specie. In order to assist in absorbing the immense mass of paper money, an issue of 25,000,000 bank notes took place, on the security of the revenues of the city of Paris, and bearing an interest of 2½ per cent. The notes which this new issue was to be the means of withdrawing were to be publicly burned. On the 10th of June, the bank was reopened for the payment of small notes—notes of 10 livres and a little upward. As almost all the population of Paris rushed to the bank to exchange their small notes for specie, the avenues to the building were blocked up, and hardly a day passed in which five or six persons were not crushed to death and trampled under foot. Silver becoming scarce, the bank was obliged to cash the notes in copper; and persons might be seen toiling along with immense loads of copper money, which they had procured in exchange for notes—glad, however, that they had got anything at all. As the old notes did not come in so fast in exchange for the new ones as was expected, fresh measures were adopted to attract them. Upwards of 30,000,000 of perpetual annuities and 4,000,000 of life annuities were created purchasable by notes; and if the people had responded to the invitation and purchased the annuities, 2,000,000,000 of the notes would have been retired in this way; but, notwithstanding the eagerness that prevailed to get rid of the notes, the terms of the offer were so unfavorable that people still hesitated and preferred keeping the notes and taking the chance of what might yet occur. To counteract this hesitation a decree was published on the 15th of August, declaring that all notes of 10,000 or of 1000 livres should have no currency except in the purchase of the annuities; but as the hesitation still continued, another decree was passed, declaring that notes would be good for no purpose whatever after the 1st of November, 1720. Numbers, however, kept their notes even after the specified time in the vain hope of better terms; and the consequence was that large quantities of Law's notes remained in houses as family lumber, down even to the date of the French Revolution, when they were produced as curiosities to be compared with the assignats."

OUR OWN BUBBLES.

Now it is not likely that the folly of France, crazed as she was by Law's plausible sophistries, will ever be repeated. It must be confessed that we have men in public life, calling themselves statesmen, whose financial theories are quite as unsound and as dangerous as his; but the world is wiser now than it was in the early part of the eighteenth century, and the mass of the American people know certainly that the law cannot make money; that values cannot be created by acts of Congress; that paper is worth precisely what it genuinely represents and no more. In this knowledge we have a safeguard against all direct attempts, upon a large scale at least, to create wealth by the issue of promises to pay. But we are, nevertheless, beset by the dangers incident to false theories of finance.

There are other ways of falling into Law's error, and in many of these ways we are constantly falling into it, if not as a whole people at least as individuals. Bubble companies exist all around us. Bubble enterprises have been pressed upon our attention as sound undertakings for a dozen years past. Many of them fell in the panic of 1873, and their fall brought sore distress to many thousands of people who had been deceived by the seeming soundness of the reasoning on which they rested. But the end is not yet. The American people have spent more money than they have made during the last ten years, and the future must make good the deficit. It is as true of communities as of individuals, that the limit of earning is the limit of safe expenditure, and the danger lies in the fact that, for a time, excessive expenditure, in the case of communities, may be concealed by the various devices of commercial credit.

Every business man knows how individuals sometimes attempt to accomplish the same end by the process known in the commercial world as "kite flying," and yet when great corporations fly kites, even business men are sometimes deceived into the belief that there is ultimate security somewhere back of the double or triple or quadruple system of hypothecation. The panic of 1873 induced a salutary caution, and it is not so easy just now as it was a few years ago, to sell the "seven-thirty gold bonds" of unbuilt or partially built railroads which, when finished, are to run, as a Congressman once put it, "through thousands of miles of trackless wilderness, where naught is heard save the scream of the savage and the howl of the wild beast." But there are bubble bonds still on the market.

There are still temptations enough for small and large investors, and hence the owner of small or moderate sums of money cannot exercise too much caution in choosing investments. Let him remember that the principle is the same in all cases, however details may differ; that money is worth no more than the market rate; that borrowers who pay more, either directly as interest, or indirectly by selling their bonds for less than their face, do so because they are not *safe* borrowers; that really sound and safe securities do not go begging for purchasers; that high interest is paid only *as a compensation for poor security.* Except in the case of very temporary commercial arrangements, with which we have nothing to do here, there can never be any other reason for paying more than the market price for the use of money, and whoever pays more does so because the security he offers is not a good one.

Bankers call a certain class of investments "women's securities," for the reason that cautious bankers always advise their purchase by people having the money of widows or single women to invest. They are eminently *safe* securities, and their absolute safety is, in such cases, a full compensation for the smallness of the interest they bear. Now for people who have saved a little money by close economy, there can be no better course than to put it into "women's securities,"—namely, government bonds and the stock of some well-managed, steady-going corporations. These are always worth their cost; they pay a small interest punctually and surely; and they are perfectly safe. There is not the smallest chance of speculation in the purchase of such securities, but there is perfect safety, which, to people not stock-jobbers, is greatly better.

THE QUESTION OF CONVERTIBILITY.

The third point to be considered in determining how savings shall be invested is the question of convertibility. Shall we put our money where we can readily reconvert it into money or where such reconversion will require time and involve trouble? The answer to this will depend upon the circumstances and character of the investor. If you know yourself to be weak of purpose and likely to spend money unnecessarily upon impulse, you owe it to yourself to place as many obstacles as possible in your own way in this matter; to fortify your purpose by every means in your power; and it will be greatly better, in such a case, to put your savings where you cannot readily get at them for the purpose of spending them. Invest them in land, or in some other way put them out of easy reach, so that no temporary pressure of circumstances may induce you to spend the money you have laid away.

Except in cases of this kind, however, there are many advantages in keeping one's money within easy control, and, other things being equal, those investments are best which leave the investor free at any time to recall his money into his own hands.

But it is not every one who can safely trust himself with this power over money of which he is likely to feel the need constantly. It is not every one whose self-mastery is sufficient to guard to day's savings against to morrow's desire to spend; and so, as it seems to me, the savings banks would fulfil their mission much better, if they would uniformly enforce their rule against the withdrawal of deposits on demand. People who need the encouragements offered by these institutions to induce them to save money, are apt to need all possible inducements to keep their savings.

These are the general principles which should govern the investment of savings for the purpose of making them earn interest. We pass now to the consideration of a subject likely to engage the attention of every man of family, namely, the purchase of a home.

SHALL WE BUY OR RENT?

There is a good deal of nonsense talked every day on the subject of owning one's home. A good deal of not very wholesome sentiment concerning it, finds its way into the columns of the weekly newspapers, and it is especially important to guard against sentimental illusions in deciding a question which, to people of limited means, is one of vital importance.

It is certainly true that there is great comfort in owning one's home,—if one is really able to own it. It is true, too, that renting is rather more expensive than owning, though the difference, in this respect, is smaller than we are apt to imagine. Interest on the cost of a house, taxes, the expense of repairs, insurance, etc., amount to very little less than rent in most cases, so that the economy of owning is not very great. The moral effect is worth more, perhaps, even in a pecuniary way, and there can be no doubt that every man *who can afford* to own his home should do so. But can you afford it? This is a question not always easily answered even when the purchase money is already in possession, and it is worth while, before purchasing, to weigh well the facts.

At the first glance it would seem evident enough that any one able to pay cash for a home, and own it free of debt, can afford to live in his house and ought to do so ; but this is not necessarily the case, and there are many instances in which even absolute and debt-free ownership has wrought disaster in men's affairs. In the first place, the owner of a home must of necessity take upon himself some portion of the risk incident to ownership. His house may be destroyed by fire, and while insurance protects him in some measure, it affords only an incomplete protection. The destruction of his home must entail considerable loss upon him, and only those who can afford to take the risk of such loss can afford to own their residence.

A more important consideration, however, is the withdrawal of money from one's business for the purpose of buying a house. Nearly all young men, and a great many of the older ones, sorely need more capital than they can command, for the successful prosecution of their business, wherefore it is simply suicidal to invest in a residence the funds which are necessary to the prosperity of one's business. The ownership of a home seriously embarrasses many a business man, and oftentimes makes utterly profitless a business which else might have brought permanent prosperity to its head. It is impossible to lay down any general rule for the reader's guidance in this matter, even if a rule were likely to be generally followed. I can only call attention to the principle, which is that you cannot afford to buy a home with money which you need in your business, and that it is in the last degree dangerous to attempt it.

MORTGAGED HOUSES.

Still more dangerous is the common practice of buying houses on credit and paying for them by instalments. That this is the easiest way of purchasing there can be no doubt, and in many cases the making of such a purchase is the very wisest thing that can be done, inasmuch as the necessity of meeting payments acts as a sharp stimulus to exertion and economy, strengthening a weak resolution to save, and checking a tendency to spend which otherwise might be irresistible. In such cases no considerations of prudence should be allowed to stand in the way of the purchaser. The man who cannot control his disposition to spend his money as fast as he makes it, takes no real risk in buying a house on these terms. If he fails in the end, and loses what he has paid, he is no worse off than if he had refrained from buying and had spent his money in other ways; while if he succeeds in paying for the house he will have bought it, practically for nothing.

But to people able to save without an inducement of this sort, such a purchase is attended with some dangers. The death of the producing member of the family, before the final payments are made, or any other occurrence which stops the income in whole or in considerable part, may cause the loss of all that has been paid, just when such loss is most insupportable.

This danger may be guarded against, so far, at least, as the *death* of the producing member is concerned, by the taking out of an extra policy of life insurance for an amount equal to the unpaid purchase money. In that case the failure of anticipated production by the death of the producer, is offset by the maturing of a life insurance policy. In other words, the risk of losing the payments made in consequence of the death of the head of the family, may be transferred from the family to a life insurance company, and prudence dictates that it should be so transferred in every case. Prolonged sickness, business failure and other mishaps are not so easily provided for, and the danger of falling upon them must remain a danger.

THE ADVANTAGES OF BUYING.

These dangers are very often overlooked, and even when the would-be owner of a house sees them, he is apt to put his fears aside as idle ones, attaching little importance to them. Or, admitting the existence of the danger as a general rule, he may, after the manner of most men, persuade himself that he is in some way exempt from the common liability to such occurrences. For these reasons I have thought it best to present this side of the matter first. The advantages of owning one's house are so apparent as hardly to need stating at all. One who lives in his own house is better settled than he could otherwise be. He is independent of landlords and free from the necessity of providing at stated periods for the payment of rent. He is exempt from the necessity of frequently removing at considerable cost, from one house to another. He has every incentive to improve and beautify and ornament his home, knowing that he is adding beauty and value to his own, and not to another's property. The moral effect upon himself and his family is by no means small, a fact so well recognized in business circles that the ownership of a home positively strengthens one's credit and improves his commercial standing.

BUYING A HOME AS AN INVESTMENT

In addition to all this it should be borne in mind that if judgment be used in the purchase the homestead will steadily grow in value, so that in the end, the investment will prove a positively profitable one. After the death of the head of the family it often becomes necessary to sell the house, and if this can be made to bring into the family treasury a good deal more money than was paid for the place, that which is sometimes the sorest of misfortunes may be converted into a positive benefit.

WHERE TO BUY.

This possibility of increasing value should be considered when the purchase is made. The house should be so chosen as to make its growth in value as certain as possible. Around growing towns it is best to choose a place a little way out, so that the natural growth of the town may inure to your benefit. It is well to remember that in ordinary cases there is a limit to the rise of property-prices in the middle of a prosperous town. When a certain point is reached people neglect the high priced lots in town for the cheaper ones in the outskirts, and so there is very much better prospect of improvement of prices in the suburbs than in the town itself, particularly if the suburbs happen to afford good villa sites. Merchants, manufacturers, lawyers, and other people in thriving towns, grow rich after a while, and as soon as they do that they are sure to set up new residences in the outskirts. This at once stimulates the prices of land there, and even if you do not need or care to sell, you are richer by just so much as your property has increased in market value.

HOW TO SECURE THE PROFIT OF YOUR INVESTMENT.

But in buying a house one naturally and properly hopes to retain it always, without the necessity of selling. The moral value of ownership is largely dependent upon this feeling of permanence; and if possible, the home once bought should be kept. But the profit incident to the advance in price, may be secured and turned into actual money while the house remains untouched. In buying, you have only to buy more land than you want, and where land is cheap, as it usually is in some part of a town's outskirts, this may be done easily enough. Your house should be so placed that the land may be divided at any time, and after you have enjoyed the use of more ground room than you need, for ten or a dozen years, a time is nearly sure to come when you may sell off the unnecessary part at a handsome profit. In the vicinity of New York, where the overflow from the city has covered every available spot for scores of miles in all directions, many men have secured homes at little cost or no cost at all by the exercise of good judgment in this way. Let me tell

ONE MAN'S STORY

as an illustration. B—— was a merchant's clerk, whose income was not greatly in excess of his absolutely necessary expenses. He bought two acres of ground in one of the New Jersey towns near the city, agreeing to pay eight hundred dollars for it, in monthly instalments of twenty dollars each, with interest at seven per cent. A building lot was all he wanted, but he knew that he could never pay for a house out of his earnings, and it was his plan to make a house by his investment. By close economy he succeeded in paying for the land in about two years, having anticipated payments whenever he could. He managed, a little later, to dig his cellar and build his foundation wall. Meanwhile his land had enhanced in value, and was worth nearly two thousand dollars. He was unwilling to sell any part of it yet, however, but he had no difficulty in borrowing four thousand dollars upon mortgage, the money to be given him as he should need it in the building of his house. The land alone was worth about two thousand dollars, and with a house worth four thousand on it, it was of course good security for more than the loan. He built his house thus with borrowed money, and moved in, thereby lessening his expenses somewhat, by saving rent and cultivating his own garden. Three years later, while his mortgage had still nearly two years to run, he sold all the land except the lot upon which his house stood for five thousand four hundred dollars, paid his debt, and found himself the owner of a comfortable sum of money, besides a house and lot worth five or six thousand dollars. For this he had actually paid only about a thousand dollars, saved out of his earnings. He had thus accomplished by a bit of good management what he never could have accomplished by direct effort.

Scores of similar cases have occurred around the metropolis, and something like this may be done in the neighborhood of almost any growing, prosperous city. If the additional land cannot be made to pay for the house, it may at least be made to help, and in any case it is well worth while to bear the possibility in mind in buying. If you build your house, build it upon as large a lot as you conveniently can, and so place it that you will be free to sell some part of it if you shall ever have occasion to do so. If you buy a house already built, buy the lot or two next to it, if it be in any way practicable to do so. If you never have occasion to sell, it will not embarrass or trouble you in any way to have the extra ground. Build or buy where the growth of your town is likeliest to benefit your property, and if you never have occasion to sell you will at least be richer by reason of the greater market value of your homestead.

CHAPTER VII.

LIFE INSURANCE.

THE PURPOSE OF THE CHAPTER.

THERE has been so much said and written of late years with respect to life insurance, that I should be tempted to omit this chapter entirely, if I were not convinced that there is still a necessity, in a treatise of this sort, for an unbiassed consideration of the practical questions on the subject, which present themselves to every married man of limited means. The pamphlets, circulars, and newspaper articles put forth, and the button-hole orations delivered to every man by canvassing agents, are the work of people who have a direct pecuniary interest in persuading their readers or hearers to insure to as large an extent and in as expensive a way as possible. The solicitor's compensation is regulated solely by the amount of the premium paid, and hence it is his interest, his business, to induce every man to insure; to persuade each to insure for as large a sum as possible; and to commend to each the more expensive rather than the cheaper forms of policies. For this reason the agent's presentation of the case is not always trustworthy, and even if it were so in the main, the fact that he stands to the subject in the relation of an advocate,—that he is a "party in interest," as the lawyers say,—greatly weakens the effect of his arguments, however excellent they may be in fact.

Without question it is the duty of well-nigh everybody to provide, by life insurance methods, against contingencies; but it is equally unquestionable that the advice of agents and other interested persons, is sometimes bad and often dangerous. It seems worth while, therefore, to examine the matter briefly, and ascertain the principles which should govern the reader in determining his course in the matter. I shall endeavor, in doing this, to look at the subject from the reader's point of view; and to point out as well as I can, the mistakes into which he is in danger of failing.

WHAT IS LIFE INSURANCE?

It would seem that everybody ought by this time to know certainly what the thing is, about which there has been so much said and written, but there is, after all, reason to doubt whether most people really do understand it. In the hands of a skilled and enthusiastic solicitor, it assumes the shape of a beneficent genius, able so to conjure with figures as to convert ridiculously small sums of money into astonishingly large ones by some sort of financial alchemy not very easily guessed at. To many it seems at least a marvellously productive system of investment, while there are incredulous others who are half inclined to reject it altogether as a preposterous device for the creation of something out of nothing, or for the delusion of unsuspecting persons. In fact it is none of these things. The life insurance company literally gives no more than it receives. It creates no wealth, and undertakes to create none. It is no financial necromancer, and it promises nothing more than it can accomplish by plain business methods. Moreover, life insurance is not an especially profitable investment, reckoning the returns it makes for the money it receives. The premiums paid on an average, would make more than the faces of the policies they represent, if kept at interest during the average lifetime of the persons insured. In other words, if one could be sure of life during the period known as his "expectation," which is simply the average period during which people of his age live, he could put his annual premiums out to better advantage than he does where he insures. Placed at interest, and the interest annually reinvested, they would yield more than the amount which the life insurance company undertakes to return at death.

WHY SHOULD YOU INSURE?

But no man can know how long he is to live, and if he should die before the average time, the sum he set out to accumulate in this way would not be forthcoming. He must take the risk of his own death, which may come at any time, and if his property is insufficient for the support of his family, he cannot afford to take such a risk. He wishes, for instance, to leave his family five thousand dollars at his death. So long as he lives he can provide for his wife and children, but at his death they must have some other resource, and this he purposes to provide in the shape of a sum of money. How is he to do it? He may put away, at interest, every year, the amount of the premium charged on a life policy, reinvesting all its interest, and if he lives as long as men of his age do on an average, the fund will exceed the desired amount. But there is a chance that he may not live so long, and in that event he must fail in his effort and leave those dependent upon him without the provision he had purposed making for them. Now it is against this chance and this only that ordinary life insurance is intended to provide. While it is impossible to say how long any one man will live, we know certainly what the average life of a thousand men of any given age will be, and the life insurance companies take advantage of this certain knowledge and by clubbing together the sums each must put away annually in order that at the end of this average time each may have the desired sum, it may with perfect safety, guaranty the amount to each. It bases all its calculations upon this, but to guard against all possible chances, it assumes four or four and one-half per cent. as the interest rate it will be able to get, while in point of fact it can always get more for the money paid it as premiums. Further, it exacts a somewhat larger premium than even this safe calculation requires. The lapsing of a good many policies, gives additional security to those which remain, and with all these safeguards there is absolutely no risk at all in the business of life insurance, properly conducted. It is assumed, in the first place, that the average life of those insured will not exceed the average of the whole community, although every precaution is taken to exclude from the company all the sickly, unsound people, who greatly diminish the community's average; it is assumed also that the money placed in the company's hands will earn no more than four or four and a half per cent., while in fact it earns half as much more; it is assumed that all the policies issued will mature and become a charge on the company, while in truth a very large number of them are abandoned altogether after one or more premiums have been paid upon them; and lastly, every premium is made greater than it need be to produce the sum expected of it.

Agents soliciting business sometimes assert and even endeavor to prove, that life insurance, considered solely as an investment, is better than any other or than most others; but this is not true, as any one may discover by a very simple arithmetical calculation, and it is altogether to the credit of the system that it does not offer special inducements in this way. Its mission is of another sort, and to fulfil that properly it must keep all the margins of safety on the side of the company. To make life insurance profitable as an investment, we must make it untrustworthy as insurance. Let it be borne in mind, then, that the only object one should have, in insuring, is to provide certainly for those dependent upon him. He can invest money much more profitably in other ways, and the only good reason he can have for insuring, lies in the fact that he cannot know how long he will live. But this is reason enough. Here is a chance of disaster against which it is his duty to provide, and it is by life insurance only that he can accomplish this all important end. It may be safely said, therefore, that every man who has others depending upon him, and whose property is not in itself adequate provision for them in the event of his death, is *in duty bound to insure his life*, not as an investment, for he can make greatly better ones, but simply as a precaution against possible disaster.

It is, perhaps, worth while to add that life insurance has a distinct value in the compulsion it puts one under to save. When a policy has once been written and a premium or two paid upon it, one is very strongly impressed with the necessity of continuing the payments, even at cost of considerable self-denial, and in this way persons who find it difficult to save anything may create an incentive to economy which they greatly need.

It is clear enough, however, in any case, that no man who has others dependent upon his exertions for comfortable support can afford, or has a right, to neglect the opportunity which life insurance affords of providing for his family in the event of his death, and so making actual and certain a considerable share, at least, of the results which he has reason to hope for from his lifetime's work.

HOW TO INSURE.

But there are right ways and wrong ways of attending to this duty and accomplishing this end, and so far at least as my observation extends, the wrong ways are more frequently followed than the right ones, chiefly because life insurance solicitors find it profitable to themselves to urge the wrong sort of policies upon their clients. I purpose, therefore, in this section, to explain, briefly, the advantages and disadvantages of the principal kinds of policies in use, and to show the dangers attending an erroneous choice. To do this properly, it is necessary first to say a word with regard to the mode by which the amount of the premiums is determined.

A careful examination of statistics has taught actuaries not only what the average life of men of any given age is and must be, but also precisely what is one man's chance of death during each year. If, for example, it is found that of a thousand men of a given age five die within the year, then the chances of death, in any individual case, are as five to one thousand, or one in two hundred. Now in such a case the actual net premium required to insure the lives of these people for one year would be five dollars for every thousand dollars of insurance. This, of course, is a statement of the problem in its simplest elements, leaving out of the account the interest which the premium will earn, as well as the expenses incurred in carrying on the business, the amount usually added for the sake of perfect safety, etc., etc. I use it in this form simply for the sake of convenience in illustrating the point, which is that the actuary may determine, with absolute certainty and accuracy, how much money each one of a thousand or of ten thousand men of any given age, must pay into a common fund, to insure the life of each for one year, and the sum thus ascertained (all the factors being admitted to the calculation) is the first year's premium. But the chances of death increase with every year of age, and hence the premium must increase in precisely the same proportion, and, to guard against this, a calculation of the average premium during the life expectancy is made, and this average premium, greater than the actual one of the early years, and less than that of the later years, is fixed upon as the amount to be paid every year, from first to last, in lieu of a series of steadily increasing and at last very burdensome annual payments. In this way the matter is greatly simplified in practice, and the difficulty of carrying insurance lessened, while by collecting more than is necessary during the early years, the company secures to itself a considerable margin of profit on those policies which shall be allowed to lapse before maturity.

The simplest form of policy in common use is one on which these average annual premiums are to continue throughout the life of the person insured, and the amount for which he is insured is to become due at his death. This is life insurance pure and simple, and as the premiums in this case are spread over the greatest possible length of time, a policy of this kind demands a smaller annual payment than any other possibly can. In determining the average the whole period of expectancy has been adopted as the basis.

Next come policies payable at death, the premiums on which are to continue not during the whole life of the person insured, but during a specific number of years,—five, ten or twenty, usually—if he live so long. The premiums in this case are ascertained by a calculation of chances precisely like that already explained; but in this case, as the premium payments are to be continued during a smaller number of years they must of course be proportionally larger while they do continue.

These are the only kinds of pure life insurance policies in common use, the only ones in which insurance alone is sought and secured. But of late years various other things have been combined with life insurance, so that in practice a very large share of the business done under the name of insurance is, in reality, insurance *plus* something else,—and the something else must be paid for in every case. This is done principally by what are called endowment policies; namely policies on which the premiums are to be paid annually either during a term of years or until the maturity of the policy; and the amount of the insurance is to be paid to the insured when he shall attain a specified age, or to those in whose behalf the policy is issued, at his death, if he shall happen to die before reaching that age. An example will make this plainer, perhaps, than any general statement can. Let us take, by way of illustration, a ten annual payment endowment policy for ten thousand dollars, payable at death or at the age of fifty years. The amount of the annual premium will depend upon the age of the applicant, but whatever it may be, he agrees to pay that premium annually during ten years. If he die at any time before reaching the age of fifty, the ten thousand dollars becomes due at once, and must be paid to the person named in the policy as the beneficiary. At the age of fifty, if he live to attain it, the amount must be paid to the person himself on whose life the policy was taken. There are other forms of endowment policies in use, but in principle they are all identical. Their value is manifest and unquestioned, and while there are cases enough in which it is best to secure, in this way, the endowment of one's later years, I am satisfied that in the great majority of instances policies of this kind are not to be recommended, particularly to young men of family, for reasons which will presently appear.

THE OBJECT SOUGHT IN INSURING.

The principal object sought in insuring one's life, is the primary one of providing for one's family in the event of death. Every man of family is in honor, and conscience, and duty, bound to secure this if he can. It is quite as imperatively his duty to provide for the comfortable maintenance of those depending upon him, after his own death, as it is to support them during his life. He has no more moral right to fail in the one duty than in the other, and the poorer he is the greater is the necessity upon him of accomplishing, by means of life insurance, that which he cannot accomplish in any other way. To secure the family from want in the event of your own death, is, I say, the primary object of life insurance; and as a matter of course this end should never be sacrificed, either in whole or in part, for the sake of less imperatively necessary objects. It is your first duty, in the matter, to secure insurance for an amount sufficient to make the comfort of your family and education of your children as certain as human affairs can be. Now if your ability to pay premiums be limited, as it is in most cases, and particularly in the cases of those for whose use this little volume is written, you cannot afford to take an endowment policy. Such policies involve insurance and *something else.* The "something else" is costly, —more costly sometimes than the insurance,—and if you cannot afford to pay for it, you have no right to purchase it. That it is a good and desirable thing there can be no doubt whatever. But so is a costly house, and so are a hundred other things that you cannot afford to buy. In this matter of life insurance there are several reasons why you may not be able to buy endowment with your insurance. The first and principal difficulty is that by taking this kind of policy you may be compelled, on account of the higher premium rates involved, to insure for a less amount than your duty to your family requires, and where this is the case, you cannot take an endowment policy without manifestly wronging those for whose benefit you are insuring, and deliberately defeating the very purpose which life insurance is designed to serve. Even when this is not the case, however—when you find it possible to take an endowment policy for the full amount which you desire to leave your family, it may be bad policy to do so. The payment of heavy premiums may very seriously embarrass your business operations, or it may so far reduce your income as to compel a system of economy hurtful to your children in moral, mental, or physical respects. In short, you may be abundantly able to purchase insurance, and yet not able, with justice to those dependent upon you, to buy with it, an endowment for yourself.

ANOTHER OBJECTION.

In addition to the possibility of working a selfish injustice to others by taking an endowment policy instead of buying only insurance, it is altogether likely, if you are a man of ordinary energy and capacity, that you will not need the endowment, when it shall fall due, half as badly as you now need the money you must now pay for it. In this country the presumption is a strong one, that a man of intelligence, sobriety and industry, will find himself in tolerably comfortable circumstance sat the age of fifty or sixty, and while even then an additional sum of five or ten thousand dollars is very desirable, it is rarely ever worth what such a sum secured by endowment policy has cost.

THE CHIEF OBJECTION TO ENDOWMENT POLICIES.

But the strongest reason of all for refusing to buy endowment with one's life insurance is that *the investment is not a profitable one.* The endowment costs more than it is worth. The money paid for it can be so invested that it will produce more than it does in this way. You can make an endowment at smaller cost than you can buy it, and the chance of premature death, which justifies investments in life insurance, does not in any way affect the present question, because in the event of death you get no endowment at all, but only insurance. By mingling insurance with endowment the companies manage to hide the fact that the purchaser of an endowment pays more for it than he would if he should create it himself, by putting its price out at compound interest; but the fact remains and must always remain, for the reason that considerations of safety compel all life insurance companies to assume, as a basis of calculation, a rate of interest considerably below that which is actually and easily secured, and to keep on the hither side of some other important margins.

I do not wholly condemn the endowment system, by any means. There are many persons whose circumstances, temperament, etc., make it advisable that they shall purchase endowments, even at the price which the companies are compelled to charge for them. But as a general rule, and particularly in the cases of people likely to be interested in this little work, it is much safer and better every way to secure pure and simple life insurance.

WHAT KIND OF POLICY IS BEST.

Putting endowments wholly out of view, then, as not advisable in the great majority of cases, we have remaining just two kinds of ordinary life policies to choose between. These are: first, a policy payable at death, with premiums payable annually during life; and, second, a policy payable at death, with premiums payable annually during a term of years. The difference between these is one of premiums only. In the first the premiums are considerably smaller than in the second, but they must be paid as long as the applicant shall live, while in the other case there is a definite limit to the term during which payments are to continue.

Which of these is the better? This is a question which every one must answer for himself, because the answer should not be the same in all cases. It is only necessary here to glance at the respective advantages of each, and ascertain what are the considerations which must govern the decision.

The limited payment policy,—*i. e.*, the policy on which payments are to cease after a term of years,—has the advantage of offering a definite and certain limit to the payment of premiums. We know at the outset the aggregate of its possible cost. Every year brings its holder nearer to the time when he shall have a paid up policy, and lessens the chance of ultimate failure through inability to pay. All these advantages are well worth considering, and in very many cases they more than counterbalance their accompanying disadvantages and dangers.

It must be remembered, however, that the premiums in this kind of insurance are considerably greater than those on an all-life policy, and this brings with it some difficulties and some dangers. If it be determined to take a limited payment policy, the additional cost is apt to tempt the applicant to content himself with a smaller amount of insurance than he actually needs; and if it be the part of wisdom to insure at all, it is certainly unwise to insure for less than one's family needs. This is the objection to limited payment policies which applies in a larger number of cases than any other.

Again, the applicants for insurance are for the most part

young men, and it is often if not generally unwise for such to withdraw from their business, for insurance purposes, more money than they must, to secure their object. It will prove more profitable to most of them if they buy their insurance at the smallest possible present cost,—*i. e.*, by taking out an all-life policy,—and keep the rest of their money in active business.

There is greater chance of failure, too, with the limited payment policy than with the other. As a matter of course it is always easier to pay a small than a large sum, and the smaller one's annual premium is the surer he may be of his continued ability to meet the payments as they shall fall due. Security being the one essential thing in this matter, everything which adds to it, everything which diminishes the chances of failure, is well worth considering. If there seems the smallest danger of ultimate failure, therefore, it is clearly the applicant's duty, to guard against it by taking that kind of policy which requires the smallest annual payments.

Lastly, in our country at least, one's early years are usually one's years of struggling. If you are a person of ordinary prudence and industry, you may very safely assume that not only your money but your money-making capacity will increase as you advance toward middle life. You have every reason to hope that ten or twenty years hence you will be much better able to pay your insurance premiums than you are now, and this being the case, it seems in the last degree foolish to lay an unnecessary burden upon your years of struggling for the sake of avoiding, in later life, a charge which is likely then to be easily borne. To see the force of this you have only to look at the history of your acquaintances, during the ten or twenty years following their marriage. Hardly one of them, you will find, was as well off at marriage as now, and while most of them, ten or twenty years ago, would have sorely felt an additional expense of a hundred dollars every year, most of them are abundantly able now to meet such a payment without inconvenience.

I urge all this the more strongly for the reason that life insurance agents, whose profits depend upon the amount of premiums received, usually advocate the more costly policy with a good deal of skill, and as a result there are more mistakes in that than in the other direction. Before leaving the subject let me call attention to one additional fact bearing upon the question. The holder of an all-life policy, may at will exchange it for one of the limited payment kind, if, at any time, he shall find it desirable to do so, and hence in choosing the less burdensome one he does not necessarily bind himself to continue payments during the whole term of his natural life. He reserves to himself in fact, all the rights which he would have in the other case.

FOR HOW MUCH OUGHT ONE TO INSURE?

If it be one's duty to insure at all, it is his duty to insure for an amount sufficient to provide for the comfort and welfare of his family after his death, if he possibly can ; and if that be impossible, he is clearly bound to secure as much insurance as he can "carry." But beyond this there is grave reason to question the value of life insurance, and it is the opinion of many shrewd observers that too much insurance is nearly as common as too little, among people who insure at all.

We have already seen that, considered solely as an investment, life insurance has little to recommend it, wherefore the only reason there could be for taking larger policies than one really needs, is not a good reason, and there are positive objections too, to over insurance. If the premiums amount to more than the insured person can comfortably spare from his business, the unwisdom of taking the unnecessary burden upon his shoulders is manifest. But even if this be not the case, the feeling that one's family is abundantly, and more than abundantly, provided for by insurance, is apt to breed habits of negligence in business and careless extravagance in living which may at any time work the ruin of the man, even to the extent of destroying the provision by insurance on which he has so confidently depended. It is impossible to fix any proper and definite limit in the matter, but there seems little room to doubt that over insurance is in more than one way dangerous, even when it does not result, as it often does, in inability to pay the premiums and the final loss of insurance altogether.

WHAT COMPANIES ARE BEST?

Every agent will name his own first, of course, admitting perhaps that there are a few others nearly as good. The fact is that between the well-established, conservative companies, there is little if any choice. They all base their calculations upon the same mortality tables and the same low rates of interest. They all charge practically the same premium rates, and they are all *perfectly safe.* But there are unsafe companies too. These are the ones which offer " special inducements," or undertake to unite politics or denominational theology or partisanship of some other sort with business, appealing to prejudice for patronage. The public has had one sharp example of the folly of listening to appeals of this sort, and I need only caution the reader in general terms to beware of every man and every company which offers to do the business of life insurance on any but the strictest and most conservative business principles. Men who ask credit or patronage on the strength of their theological opinions, or their political leanings, and men who offer to take risks of any sort for a smaller compensation than the nature of the risks justifies, are to be shunned in any business; and especially dangerous are such people in a matter like life insurance, in which perfect security is the one thing needful. When you insure your life your object is to provide a certain sum of money for your family after your death, and you cannot afford to endanger the end for the sake either of gratifying a prejudice or of gaining some small present advantage. Dividends and other inducements of that kind, are of small account at best, and are for the most part illusory. Every sound company does business at fair safe rates; the cost is almost exactly the same in all of them; and whatever agents may urge as regards low rates, participation in profits, etc., etc., the fact is well established that it costs just as much to insure in one good company as in another. The important point is to beware of companies that are not good; and inasmuch as the basis of calculation is precisely the same in all companies, those that offer "special inducements" of one kind or another are doubtful ones.

www.ingramcontent.com/pod-product-compliance
Lightning Source LLC
LaVergne TN
LVHW021421110826
845150LV00007B/2027

* 9 7 8 1 4 2 5 5 0 8 8 0 7 *